OH, NO, THEY'RE ENGAGED!

A SANITY GUIDE FOR THE
MOTHER OF THE BRIDE OR GROOM

OH, NO, THEY'RE ENGAGED!

JOY SMITH

OH, NO, THEY'RE ENGAGED!
A Sanity Guide for the Mother of the Bride or Groom

Books may be ordered through booksellers or by contacting:

JSBooks Publications
http://jsbookspublications.weebly.com

Because of the dynamic nature of the internet, any web addresses or links contained in this book may have changed since publication and may no longer be valid.

Certain stock imagery © Thinkstock

ISBN: 978-0-9862422-0-5

Printed in the United States of America
First edition published 02/16/2012
JSBooks rev date: 12/05/2014

For my children.

ACKNOWLEDGMENTS

MANY THANKS TO editor Jane Haertel at Crazy Diamond for her sharp eyes and sage advice. A big smooch to my pals at the Connecticut Romance Writers of America who encouraged me never to give up. And all my love to my husband, Gil, and our three adult children. Without them, I couldn't have written this book.

TABLE OF CONTENTS

INTRODUCTION

ONGRATULATIONS! YOU'RE ABOUT TO GIVE birth again, this time to a wedding! As a parent, your life is about to change, and this will have far-reaching effects. Who could guess the spark of a tiny diamond would have the power to ignite the flurry of activities and emotions following the engagement of a daughter or son? Gaining a new family member can be as excruciating as childbirth and, ultimately, as rewarding.

As mother of the bride, you're fully involved in all the excitement, aggravations, and sentiments befitting your position. You're consulted; you play a significant role in the big event. Your schedule is plumped with a potpourri of decisions, new relationships, and a tumult of emotions. You run inane errands, clutter your home with piles of useless information, and spend an inordinate amount of time on the phone and on e-mail dealing with minutiae. You are a queen bee, your hive abuzz with activity.

Then comes your son's wedding, and the entire process seems almost anticlimactic. While his wedding is every bit as important to you as your daughter's, what looms forefront in your mind is *where do I fit in?* When dealing with a son's marriage, a mother's role is more supportive than active. Understanding that you are needed just as much, but in a different way, is paramount.

Marriage is a turning point in your son's or daughter's life, a commitment to a future as a responsible adult with a family to care for. When the reality meets the dream, I guarantee your child will rely on you for help in crossing over.

This special time in your life gifts you with closeness to your child, even as it thrills and scares you to death. Fits of activity and ever-present anxiety will terminate with the sweet pain of separation. You may not have been this "in touch" with your son or daughter since babyhood; it feels good to be needed, and it may hurt to see it end.

Yet, a child's marriage is hardly an *end*. It begins a host of new relationships—an extended family, a new daughter or son to spoil, and maybe grandchildren before long.

Oh, No, They're Engaged! will help you deal with any unexpected issues and emotions you may experience throughout the wedding planning process and give you the strength and understanding to guide your child into a new life.

Dear Joy,

Yikes! They're in lo ve—and I'm worried!

CHAPTER 1

A Proposal's on the Table

I'LL NEVER FORGET THE EVENING our son, Rick, came home hiding a smile. He reached into his pocket, drew out a small, blue velvet box, and opened it to reveal a diamond so new and shiny it made me squint. I was so thrilled for him that I did what any decent mother would do. I gave him a bear hug and cried, and then I tried on the ring.

Because a son is the ring giver, you, as a parent, are apt to be more involved in the proposal process, especially if he is still living at home. Getting married is a financial decision as well as an emotional one. Before our son became engaged, he anguished over what to do. Was this the right time for him, and where would he buy a ring he could afford?

With a daughter, you are on the receiving end waiting for that moment when the guy she's either been living with or dating for some time coughs up a commitment. It's nice if a guy asks permission to marry your daughter, but this is not always the case. Don't expect. Just accept and enjoy. Your young couple may come bubbling through the door to announce their happiness and flaunt a ring, or you and your spouse may learn of the pending engagement in advance and be saddled with keeping the secret, as we were.

One weeknight, John showed up at our house in Connecticut around dinnertime. My husband and I peered out the window, not understanding what he was doing there, while our daughter, Mary, was in Boston. He made us feel special by asking our permission to marry her. I fed John our son's steak dinner (Rick had to settle for leftovers). Two years later, when daughter number two's long-time boyfriend roared up our driveway in the same manner, my husband and I hi-fived. I snagged an extra pork chop from the freezer and nuked another potato. In both instances, my husband and I were sworn to secrecy until our future sons-in-law could properly present the rings to our daughters. Secrets, particularly happy ones, are hard to keep.

> *Young men in the Hopi tribe would propose by preparing a bundle of fine clothing and white buckskin moccasins and leaving it on a maiden's doorstep. If the woman accepted his bundle, it meant she agreed to marry him.* [1]

Now, let's talk about this ring-on-the-finger thing. Rings symbolize eternal love, but does a guy really have to give a girl a ring to become engaged? Of course not. This is one of many traditions that have become grounded in advertising—"What's a few month's paycheck towards the rest of your life?"

He's not buying her, for goodness sake, he's asking her to marry him!

A huge diamond may last forever, but that doesn't mean the marriage will. The diamond is a symbol, not a necessity—the same goes for the wedding ring. In the case of a daughter, gracefully accept whatever has been given to her as a symbol of engagement; it may only be a promise. A tiny stone, or none at all, doesn't mean the guy loves your daughter less. My parents took their vows using a cigar band and their marriage lasted until death did them part.

> *The custom of the engagement ring began with the Anglo Saxons. The gift of a ring was a token of promised love, its circular band a symbol of eternal love and unity. Later, the enduring qualities of a diamond came to represent the strength of never-ending love.* [2]

But you're concerned . . .

Once the ring is on the finger, reality may strike. Your son's unmarried buddies are pooh-poohing the whole business, or you and your husband aren't thrilled with your prospective son-in-law for a variety of reasons—some serious, some just plain picky. This is the time to keep communications flowing between you and your son or daughter. Don't criticize, just listen. If asked, offer advice with as much objectivity as you can muster. Do remember that your role as a controlling parent diminished as soon as your son or daughter became an adult. Here are some situations you may run into:

Ring around the finger?

. . . or is it through the nose? Guys will be guys, but a common problem is the buddy system. When your son proposes, his friends may try to convince him he is giving up his freedom. Should you learn your son has been listening to his friends instead of to his heart, speak to him about it. Better yet, ask Dad to help him understand the sow-the-wild-oats-while-you-can philosophy is merely a scare tactic that reflects immaturity, rather than common sense. Marriage is a loving bond between two people, a pact to share a life. Your son's relationship with his loved one will be what they, as a couple, make it, not what others say it will be.

You don't want this marriage!

Things don't always work out the way we'd like them to. What if you never liked a particular boyfriend or girlfriend, and you like this person less now that marriage is on the horizon? Your feelings may be real and not necessarily unfounded. You suspect the guy is abusive: he tosses insults at your daughter like confetti, always putting her down. Or, that girl your son loves barely speaks to you. Will you ever see your son once they are married? The concerns go on . . .

> *He's a cheapskate.*
> *She can't cook.*
> *He can't hold down a job.*
> *She has no manners!*

Yes, we parents can be super critical, but even if our worries are justified, our influence is limited. We can suggest and advise but can no longer order change. We deal with our cards as they are dealt us, even if it means maintaining a blank face with a poor hand because it's a parent's only choice. We can always hope, once we're through playing the game, that our child either has won a suitable mate or averted a potentially bad marriage.

—Or else!

Sometimes, we're so frustrated with a situation—we hate the guy and just know the wedding will result in a disastrous life for our daughter—that we try to stop it with an ultimatum: *if you marry him, I never want to see you again*, or *you will no longer be welcome in our home*. A softer version of this might be *I'm not coming to the wedding*. Don't threaten anything you can't carry out. Better yet, don't threaten at all.

A woman I know of married a less than desirable man—arrested for dealing drugs, and couldn't hold down a job. They had lived together long enough to bear and raise a three-year-old child. When the couple finally decided to wed, the parents, who had been against their union from the get go, refused to attend the ceremony, creating bad feelings.

Before taking this type of hurtful and irrevocable step, think about what will be gained from doing so. Yes, you will have "shown them" you really are upset, made your point loud and clear. But will making threats stop the wedding? Such actions might, in fact, cause your child to dig deeper into the relationship, to ally with this partner protectively. Them against the world—*yours*.

Further, you will have abandoned your child at a crucial time. A parent's support cannot be replaced by friends. Regardless of who is right or wrong, in this thorny situation there can be only losers. You will have lost your child, either emotionally or physically, as well as the opportunity to get to know and love your grandchildren—a situation a great deal worse than you might've bargained for.

Second time around

Complex issues often surround second marriages, so it's important for you, as well as your son or daughter, to be aware of any problems resulting from the death of a spouse, a divorce, or children from a previous marriage. In the case of a widow or widower who has decided to remarry after a good relationship, prospects are good for a successful second marriage. Most problems occur when people go blindly into marriage to a divorced person without understanding why the first marriage failed. Causes can range from addictions, physical abuse, and infidelity to simple lack of compatibility. Keep your eyes and ears open and you may pick up on serious issues your son or daughter chooses to ignore. I'm not saying play traffic cop and hold up the

STOP sign; but should you sense a serious flaw in the intended, find a tactful way to open your child's eyes to it—then step back.

You may be cheering because this marriage will make you an instant grandmother, but worry about your son or daughter handling an add-on parental role in an established single-parent family. In such families, children may resent an intruder. The younger the children the easier it will be for them to accept a step-parent and a new set of grandparents. While a needy child may embrace the union, a rebellious one—especially if fueled by a jealous ex-spouse—can make life miserable for everyone. Then, there is the question of allegiance. Children may act up to command the attention of their biological parent, leaving the step-parent to feel sidelined in the relationship. These kinds of issues don't go away overnight, but call for a steady dose of patience and love.

On a positive note, you may find your son or daughter is welcomed into the new family, like my friend's son was. Seth hooked up with Alice, who has two children, ages eight and ten. I had the opportunity to see this family together before the actual engagement and, from glow of happiness surrounding them, it was easy to see they had bonded. The children were flower girl and ring bearer at the couple's wedding, and my friend and her husband are now doting grandparents.

Too old!

Perhaps you really like the guy or gal your offspring has chosen, but you've a nagging problem—their age difference is too great. If the age span is five years or less, we parents can usually deal with it. At least the couple is of the same generation.

However, if the intended is your age, you think *cradle robber*. What can he or she possibly have in common with someone that young? You cringe when you think of them having sex. What if this fellow is looking to revive youth through marrying a younger woman?

And, if it's a first marriage, what held him or her back so long? Maybe he's a mama's boy or a gigolo, or she's a lesbian? If the man's been married before and has children living elsewhere, in addition to the aforementioned issues you worry that your daughter may never have a child of her own.

While it's more common for older fellows to seek young women, there are many successful unions of older women to younger men. Still, you worry. Is your son going to be treated as a child? Is she too old to have children—denying you grandchildren? If she's your age, do you feel in competition with her for your son's love and attention?

May-December marriages can and do work out well. I know a couple who have been together for years. He's sixty-something and she's thirty. They love each other dearly, have friends of all ages, travel extensively, and own a fabulous home.

So, Mom, don't fret. The up side of an older mate is that you and Dad have gained a son or daughter-in-law who has lived through the same things you have, so bonding will be a snap. And, as long as love is true, your children will have the same good life you envision for them.

Pre-marital housekeeping

As a parent who may have waited to have sex until marriage, you may find it inappropriate to have your son or daughter living with his or her intended. Or maybe you're thinking *all those wasted years I could have been having a high old time*. Knowing how I felt about them sharing an apartment, Rick slipped a pillow and a blanket into the bathtub before my husband and I arrived for a visit. Rick claimed he slept there, while his fiancée, Lois, enjoyed the king-sized bed. Although we laughed, the scary thing is I wanted to believe my son was chaste. To save rent money, both my daughters opted to share an apartment with their respective fiancés during the months preceding their weddings. My husband and I resolved our feelings, realizing our children were smart enough pool their finances and save for their futures.

Same-sex union

The world has become more accepting of gay relationships, evidenced by the legalization of gay marriages or civil unions in some states in the U.S.A. If your child opts for a same-sex partner, forget what your friends or family will think and accept it for what it is. You can't change your child's mind, nor should you try. Your child needs your love and encouragement more than ever when he or she goes against the odds. In many cases, coping with such a situation can take a strong constitution, tight lips, and lots of love—and we all know love conquers all.

As to same-sex wedding planning, I admit I have had no direct experience in this area. However, according to Emily Post, the process is essentially the same as for a heterosexual wedding. Legally, their pairing will be considered either a civil union or a marriage, depending on the laws of the state where the wedding is to be held.

Well, the hard stuff is over. At least you hope it is. There's a proposal on the table for your daughter or your son, it doesn't matter which. A proposal means an engagement and an engagement is their first step out the door, *your* door, into a new life. If you are especially lucky, the chosen partner is smart, motivated to work hard, thinks your husband and you are great people, and would do anything in the world to make your child happy.

Now, it's time to celebrate!

Dear Joy,

This is scary. What if the prospective in-laws hate us? Do I have to put on a shindig?

CHAPTER 2
Mark the Engagement

O NCE THE ENGAGEMENT IS OFFICIAL, take steps to get the wedding off the ground by finding a special way to honor this commitment and getting to know your child's future in-laws. Also, it's never too early to begin planning the event. Should you begin to feel stressed with all the to-do's, be grateful that in modern times the bride is no longer kidnapped from her home and that you have the opportunity to participate in the wedding process.

> *Historically, men captured their brides. The prospective groom often used a warrior friend to fight off other men who wanted the woman and to prevent the woman's family from finding the couple. After the abduction, the groom would take his bride into hiding so that by the time the bride's family discovered them, the bride would already be pregnant. The couple would drink a wine made from mead and honey for a month after their marriage, hence the honey moon.[3]*

An engagement is a relationship milestone your couple will always hold dear. It's customary for the parents of the bride-to-be to announce the happy news to family and friends by phone, e-mail, or formal note. This also may include a newspaper announcement. If the parents are divorced, the mother tells all. In a formal announcement, she would make mention of the bride's father. Depending on their age and independence, the engaged couple, however, may opt to handle their own betrothal announcements.

Celebrate

Find a special way to recognize this commitment to wed. Marking the event can be as simple as a champagne toast at a family dinner. Usually, a short engagement period won't warrant a separate party, as it will be close to the wedding. Having the party a couple of months after the actual engagement will give your couple a chance to plan their lives and to think about the size and type of wedding they might want.

If your relatives get together for special occasions, choose one of these to announce your son's or daughter's engagement. Everyone will have a chance to slap the happy couple on the back or hug them, and you won't need to pay for a party. Plus you've done your family a kindness. Because it's not an official engagement party, the gift issue doesn't surface. At minimum, there will be a shower and a wedding gift for these folks to buy for your couple. We all love parties, but gift-giving gets old by the time we attend the third festivity for the same event.

I have never felt the need to host an engagement party, but then our situations never warranted one. Our family is small and tight-knit and the future in-laws lived a plane ride away. A shared dinner with the parents of your child's intended is a good way to celebrate the engagement. Establishing a relationship with the future in-laws, which we will discuss shortly, is crucial. These folks will be in your son's or daughter's life for a long time.

Having an official engagement party can be a fun way to let family and friends in on the upcoming event. Anyone can host; but, traditionally, throwing the party has been the role of the bride's parents. The key attendees are the bride, groom, their immediate families, and possibly close friends who are likely to be part of the wedding party. The type and style of the event will depend on time and money available. Take care that this event, or any other prewedding party, is not so elaborate that it will outshine the actual wedding. If your party will be somewhat formal, it's a kindness to exclude those who may not be invited to the wedding. While gifts aren't necessary, most folks will feel funny about arriving at a party empty-handed. Ask your son or daughter to put off opening any gifts received at the party for a later time to avoid embarrassing guests who chose not to bring one.

Sometimes, the groom's parents will plan a local shindig to allow friends and relatives to meet their prospective daughter-in-law. This is a nice way of providing an opportunity for those who cannot attend the wedding to congratulate the couple. Our immediate family was invited to a backyard picnic, complete with lawn games and a family Oompah band, held at our future son-in-law's home in another state. We were thrilled to meet the entire clan in one swoop—Great Grandma, elderly aunts and uncles, cousins, and friends of the family who might have never made the trip to Connecticut for the wedding.

A gift to remember

Engagement gifts are optional, usually only given by close relatives and friends of the bride and groom. I've always enjoyed giving something to commemorate the beginning of my son's or daughter's life with a mate. I couldn't help but reminisce the Thanksgiving my daughter lit candles ensconced in the crystal holders that her sister and I gave her as an engagement gift. Like these candlestick holders, a gift should be something lasting, symbolic even, an item the couple can enjoy in their new surroundings.

Choose a gift that the couple will remember you by. Almost anything can be inscribed today, from coasters and picture frames to silver platters. If the couple has selected their china and flatware patterns, give them their first place setting. They won't remember the particular pieces, but they will remember that *you* gave them their *first* ones. My daughter-in-law and son were thrilled to open a box of their china. They held each piece as if caressing it, turning it every which way to catch the light and running their fingers along the smooth, curved surface. Watching their immense pleasure for those few moments was almost as good as sex.

What if they break their engagement?

Gack. Guess you don't need to read much after this section, should this be the case. It's easier to cancel an engagement than to suffer the horrors of a divorce. So, if your child comes to you with news that the wedding is off, take it like a man (or woman). Forget about what your friends and family will think. It's not important. Simply announce the news to them by phone, with a short note, or in an e-mail message. Although you will hear the horrified "whys," "whats," and "hows," avoid the urge to explain. The breakup was not your decision, nor is it your responsibility to cover up or candy-coat for others.

Should the break-up occur after wedding invitations have been mailed, etiquette deems that the persons hosting the wedding send out cancellation notes. If your daughter asks, tell her *yes* she should return the ring unless her fiancé broke the engagement (in which case she could keep it if she wants to). It would be kind to return any ring that is a family heirloom. Also, your daughter needs to give back or replace in kind all those lovely engagement, shower, or wedding gifts, along with an explanatory note (sob).

Assuming the wedding will be forthcoming, your next step might be to connect with future in-laws—unless you have done this already.

Meet the in-laws

If the betrothed have been dating for a long time, you may have already met the guy's or gal's parents and a formal meeting won't be necessary. Etiquette books state that the groom's family should contact the bride's family soon after they hear of the engagement. If you are the mother of the bride and haven't heard a peep from the other side, don't stand on ceremony for goodness sake.

In my experience, it doesn't matter who calls whom first, as long as both parents connect. Sometimes, a son or daughter will arrange a simple meet or just hand the phone to you. While a letter or an e-mail note would establish a connection, I feel it's a cop out. This is a time of joy. Unless the prospective in-laws are unreachable—perhaps they are on a boat in the middle of the ocean—it's best to talk live with them, to break the ice and get to know them.

A simple phone call gushing over the engagement and complimenting their child will do the trick. This was always a difficult call for me to make because I just knew I was going to stumble over my words and say something dumb. *What would they think of me?* I usually wound up writing out my greeting and then reading it to get through those first awkward minutes. Then I realized these folks were just as nervous as I was. When my first daughter was to be married, I called Rose and Tim to introduce myself. They used their extension phone so they could *both* speak with me. By the time I realized this, it was too late to involve my husband, who was glued to the History Channel on television. Men have an uncanny sense of when to be *un*available, don't they?

Once both sets of parents have established they are pleased about the union and look forward to getting together, it's up to the bride's mother to suggest something. A simple occasion where you can get together and talk a bit is appropriate. Think of it as a blind date. An initial meeting place in *neither* of your homes is safest because you won't have to clean either of your houses.

Experience has taught me that going out to dinner works best because it's easy to fill awkward gaps in the conversation with browsing the menu and raving about the food. Also, you will get a feel for what types of food these people enjoy while you learn a little about them. This info will come in handy when planning the rehearsal dinner and wedding reception menus.

When my first daughter became engaged, I invited her fiancé's family to my home for dinner. Everything went beautifully. They turned out to be wonderful people, just as I expected, but the preparation for this event was nerve-racking. There were so many things I didn't know about these folks. I needed to plan a menu everyone would enjoy. These days you have to ask questions before you serve food. I squeezed tidbits of information about what they liked to eat from my daughter's fiancé. Were they vegetarians or vegans? Tea-totalers? Did they smoke? Did they suffer food allergies?

What if they didn't like us?

I felt so exposed. I dragged out my tarnished sterling flatware and decided I must use it. I spent a full morning polishing it up and, once I got going, went on to tackle the rich black patina on my mother's silver tea service. Nothing would do short of hauling out the good china, hand-tatted linens and, of course, wowing them with a gourmet meal.

Once said future in-laws arrived, I served plump shrimp and champagne while we sat stiffly in the sunken white living room we only use at Christmas, making small talk about the weather and their flight down to see us. When I get nervous, I talk. I babbled about anything and nothing.

I filled gaps in our conversation by running back and forth to the kitchen, taking deep breaths and raising the heat on the peppercorn-crusted prime rib that wasn't done yet. I served it rare, thankful the end pieces squeaked by as medium-well for the parents. Once at the dinner table, the conversation flowed (the wine did also, and that helped). We had a grand time, but I was exhausted and thankful they hadn't accepted my invitation to stay overnight at our home. What had I been thinking?

There are plenty of tense moments during the course of putting on a wedding. Why create more? When my second daughter became engaged, our family met the parents at a restaurant for a relaxing dinner out. My future son-in-law, sweetheart that he is, even insisted on picking up the tab. So, we became guests too, and that was very nice.

In addition to figuring out how best to entertain your future in-laws, some personal issues arise as to how to present yourself and your family. We want these people to see us at our best—first impressions last, but it's easy to over-think this and drive yourself nuts. As a woman, you may be concerned, as I was, about your appearance and that of family members. My husband is conservative enough to know not to wear homey jeans and a tee shirt and my other children also would dress sensibly so their appearances weren't of concern to me—but they might be for you.

I can be a bit flamboyant, so when I learned my daughter's future in-laws were very conservative, I purchased a staid pair of Pendleton plaid pants with a matching sweater. This outfit should have been perfect, but when I wore it on a test run, friends and family insisted I didn't look myself. So I settled for wearing a pair of corduroy jeans with a matching silk shirt and my dangly earrings, an ensemble I felt comfortable in for at-home entertaining.

Like me, you may try toning down your usual style and find you hardly recognize yourself when you look in the mirror. My advice to you and your family is to be yourselves. It's a role you can all handle comfortably. And of course the prospective in-laws will like you. Why wouldn't they? You've produced this wonderful, caring daughter or son they adore (at least you expect they do).

Be confident. Set inadequacies aside and concentrate on the project at hand: getting acquainted with your child's new family. Once you have survived the first phone call and first meeting, you will have established a rapport with these nice people and, depending on their proximity and how well you get along, you may even become fast friends.

What if we don't like each other?

Only in fairyland is everything sweet and nice. In a perfect world everyone lives in harmony, free of conflict, hostilities, and personality problems. It's not always easy to combine two families, especially if there are cultural or religious differences. Both may not view the world in the same way. Our differences can be wonderful, but unless we can respect the differences in others, accept them for who and what they are and how they live their lives, we risk making life miserable for those around us.

Once you've survived the initial meeting with your son's or daughter's future in-laws, you have probably formed a few opinions of them. In fairyland, they are wonderful, caring people who are flexible, sharing, and one hundred percent behind this union. In reality, they may be difficult, pushy, meddling fools. It's like a card game; sometimes you draw the king and queen of hearts, other times you get stuck with the joker or the wild card.

> *Tips for Dealing with In-laws*
> - *Be yourselves.*
> - *Accept others as they are.*
> - *Be assertive, yet flexible.*
> - *Respect your children's wishes.*
> - *Handle your own issues.*
> - *Smile, even if it hurts.*

If, after connecting with your future son or daughter-in-law's family, you feel an instant dislike, try to understand what is causing this. Are you jealous because they have a more opulent life style than yours? Or do you look down on them because they live a simpler life? Do your personalities clash? Arrogance and single-mindedness can get in the way of harmony. These people, this family, will become part of your daughter or son's life. Accept them for better or worse, just as your child must.

Too often we expect all families to be like ours and then are disappointed when they are not. Some families care too much, and some don't seem to care at all. Try not to be judgmental. Unless you've ridden in their Volkswagen (or BMW), how can you decide whether their feelings are justifiable? Accept these people as they are, and deal with any conflicts that arise with diplomacy.

When you meet your future son or daughter-in-law's parents and finish marveling over the obvious physical resemblances—the same bright blue eyes, ski-slope nose, or big ears—what is not immediately evident is their philosophy. How has the parents' way of life influenced their son or daughter?

Is the young person proud of them and wanting to be like them, or is he or she racing in the opposite direction?

Meeting future in-laws and observing their relationship with their child over time will help you to be understanding. I used to think my future daughter-in-law didn't care for me. She wasn't "huggy" like me. Once I got to know her parents and realized theirs was a "hands-off" family, I accepted this facet of her personality and made a conscious effort not to smother-mother her.

As wedding plans progress, your relationship may build with your child's future-in-laws, especially if they live nearby. You are probably in trouble if they present you with a 200-person guest list as a *fait accompli* or if the mother of the groom ignores your wishes and tries to take over. If you allow your emotions to boil over, problems are certain to occur. Beware of placing your child in an emotional tug-of-war as both sets of parents try to assert power and exert influence over an event that should be fairy-tale happy.

Likewise, hold back on interceding for your son or daughter on their issues with prospective in-laws. These folks will be part of your child's life for a long time, and the sooner he or she learns to deal with them the better. If a bride and groom can survive these and other wedding planning anxieties, they have already gone a good way towards building the type of relationship that underlies a strong alliance.

The personal feelings you have over this union will mellow over time, if you let them. What's important is not allowing your own negativity to spoil this joyous period for your child. Don't pick fights, and ignore any barbs tossed at you. None of us is perfect. Be assertive, yet flexible. Temper your prejudices, and be prepared to be as gracious as you can be whenever you are together.

Keep the children's wishes and overall happiness in the forefront. Don't make them go-betweens for conveying your problems to the in-laws. Settle your problems as directly and tactfully as possible. Your children, after all, might become addled enough to rethink this marriage thing; then what will you do with that wedding dress with the non-refundable deposit?

Dear Joy,

I want to be part of their lives, but I don't want to be a buttinski.

CHAPTER 3

Accept Change

ONCE THE RING IS ON the finger, you'll feel a shift. The boyfriend or girlfriend is going to be part of your life, whether you are happy about it or not. This change has reverberating effects. Now that you have welcomed your prospective son or daughter-in-law a host of odd questions bombard your mind, such as: *Will he want to call me "Mom"? When is her birthday? What are his sizes?* Gifts become more personal, more substantial. The ten-dollar acrylic scarf you gave your daughter's boyfriend last Christmas is upgraded to a hundred-dollar Polartec® jacket when he becomes her fiancé, and that cheapo candle for the girlfriend? Nothing but gold earrings or a cashmere sweater set will do now that she is going to become your "daughter."

Giving away a child, which is exactly what a wedding is, diminishes our parenting role and can bring on a feeling of loss. If your child is living at home and moves out to marry, the rite is coupled with the empty nest syndrome, creating a double whammy. Not only have you handed over your child, but previously filled rooms are empty and the house is quiet—too quiet.

Of course, with today's unemployment issues, the opposite situation could occur and your nest may be repopulated to include the wedded couple while they save for a place of their own. This means more laundry, larger meals—and you thought you were going to get a break from all that extra work—not to mention the screams of sexual ecstasy emanating from your child's old room. You need your rest more than they do, so set ground rules for your household and, for heaven's sake, put them in a bedroom as far away from yours as possible.

Through all this, what hurt me the most was losing my status as my daughter's primary confidante.

She's telling her fiancé things she once shared with you.

The couple becomes more inseparable than ever as they evaluate living quarters and configure their lives. If not at your home, where will they live after they marry? They are now a pair; where one goes, the other goes, too. Just before the wedding, our son-in-law's company transferred him to Raleigh, North Carolina. He and my daughter moved a plane ride away soon after their honeymoon. Daughter number two followed suit when her new husband went for his master's degree at the University of North Carolina and then took a job in the Charlotte financial industry. I will always miss having my daughters close by—even though they spoil me when I visit. Thank goodness, my son decided to stick around!

It's time to share

To make matters worse, your family is no longer primary in your son's or daughter's life. The first time your child broaches the subject of not being home for Christmas (or, Hanukkah, or Kwanzaa—you get the drift), you gasp. They are not even married, and already you are contending with dividing the time. It may take you a while to get used to this equation.

Fair is fair. Keep in mind that the future in-laws feel the same way you do. If they are nearby, the kids will try to split their time between both parents' homes. If the parents live far apart, the couple may need to alternate holidays. When it's your "on" year for Christmas, you're euphoric. When it's the in-laws' turn, you spiral into a deep funk and don't even feel like putting up a tree.

Each family has to work through its own ways of dealing with holidays without loved ones. My advice is to set your parental feelings aside and consider the stress the kids have to endure to please two or more sets of parents. Don't guilt-trip them into exhaustion. The holidays should be a peaceful, joyous time, not a circuit of road trips and double meals. If your kids can't be with you for Thanksgiving, invite them over for turkey the weekend before or after and pretend it's Thanksgiving Day. You can even tape the Macy's Parade and the football game. Run the video during dinner. Everyone will be in the spirit, and only the calendar will know for sure.

It may work out that both sets of parents can be joined in one home for a holiday. If you live in the same town or within driving distance, this can be an ideal situation. Everyone is together under one roof. The kids are in heaven because they don't have to worry or drive, and everyone has a good time. Thanksgiving at your house, Christmas dinner at theirs—the simplest solution to a classic problem.

Get involved

Once I recuperated from the shock of a forthcoming wedding, my first thought was *what shall I wear?* My husband's was *who's going to pay for everything?* With so many imminent decisions, it's natural to feel inundated with a flurry of unanswered questions. While the bride and groom are figuring out what avalanche hit them, a mother might wonder what she should be doing, and a dad's apt to feel pressured about cost.

Delivering a first wedding is like having your first baby. You worry and fret over doing everything by the book. By the time the second child is on the way to matrimony, you have developed the confidence to be less concerned about breaking a rule or doing something different. There are no rules, other than exercising simple courtesies, and there's no need to wait until the next wedding to figure this out. A wedding is a rite of passage, a single-day event that reflects the spirit of the man and woman joining in wedlock. Society is becoming more accepting of non-traditional weddings. As a result, more weddings have become unique to the couple getting married—and are much better for it.

Your level of involvement is likely to be in proportion to your monetary contribution to the event. If you are paying for the wedding, or part of it, you have some say and are apt to be part of the planning process. If the couple is financing their wedding, keep your mouth shut and be grateful they are inviting you.

It's difficult to take the rumble seat when such a monumental event is going on in your child's life; but, this is not *your* wedding. It's your son's or daughter's. Resist the urge to be a control freak. Your child doesn't need added pressure or aggravation during the highly charged span of time between engagement and wedding. Spend some time discussing the type of wedding the couple envisions and offer your help.

As mother of the bride there is much to do, because you normally would take the parental lead. Officially, you are considered part of the wedding party. Should the bride do the bulk of the planning, she, no doubt, will rely on comfortable old Mom for advice in working out the details. When a son gets married, a mother's role is secondary; you and your husband are merely esteemed guests.

For me, being mother of the groom felt odd after holding court over two daughters' weddings, a combination of letdown and relief. While it was nice not to have as much responsibility, being a spectator was agonizing. Marrying off our son was just as heart-wrenching as giving away our daughters. It was difficult to hold back, to not butt in with my opinions and thoughts until I was asked.

Obviously, there are exceptions. If the son's parents are paying for the wedding, they will become the primary parental interface for the planning. Likewise, if the wedding is held in the hometown of the son and the bride's family lives far away, the mother of the groom may take on many of the responsibilities.

A friend's son married a girl whose mom wasn't around. She helped pick out the girl's gown and made all the arrangements for a splendid wedding. Being willing to give of your time, money, and—most importantly—of yourself is a wonderful way to strengthen the bond between you and your future daughter or son-in-law. So, when the opportunity arises to assist in wedding-related events, make it a point to be available. You won't be sorry you expended the extra effort.

You are their touchstone

No matter how little or how much you participate, understand you are not simply planning a wedding. You are the tree that supports your children as they prepare to branch out and make massive changes to their lives.

If your son or daughter has been on his or her own for a while, there may be second thoughts about loss of independence. A marriage is sharing more than a bed. It's sharing bank accounts, possessions, and time. Refer your child to the section on marriage in *The Prophet* by Kahlil Gibran[4], a book that was popular in the sixties. The gist of it is, each person in a relationship (marriage) is an individual and should retain this while helping the other to become stronger. Quotes from this book have become integral to many wedding ceremonies.

The couple's lives will be intertwined, but that doesn't mean that a daughter can't spend a night out with the girls or a son shouldn't get together with his friends for a golf game on a Saturday afternoon. The relationship they have formed premarriage is an indicator of what's to come.

My son had been dating Lois since high school. As their senior year of college neared, they broke up by mutual agreement to check out what and who else was out there. My son, Rick, took the rift in their relationship hard. He lost weight, slept little, and spent the next six months in a deep depression. As parents, there was little my husband and I could do except reassure him and encourage him to date others and to try new things.

I was thrilled the day my son showed up at my office, hand in hand with Lois. "I have my Lois back," he said. We all cried and hugged. The crux of the breakup was not looking for love in other places, but that Lois felt tied down, that she was no longer her own person. Because she and my son always did everything together, she had given up seeing her friends or doing her own thing. When she and my son reformed their relationship, it was on a different plane, which lasts to this day. They take turns pursuing personal goals. Rick spends a golf weekend in Hilton Head with the guys, and Lois takes a drive to Boston to visit her girlfriend.

Having children (four cuties, now) has slowed this down. Independent weekends have shrunken to a few stolen hours here and there. What's important is this couple understands each other's need for time alone, as well as time with friends, minus the guilt of independence. I've watched this relationship grow and develop. It is strong, stronger than most. Maybe we should all take a lesson from Lois.

Dear Joy,

Lord help me. They want a circus for a wedding!

CHAPTER 4
Start Wedding Planning

ONCE A WEDDING IS IN the offing, my first stop has always been the bookstore, where I buy the prospective bride a wedding planning guide and snatch up one each of the current bridal magazines—costly things, aren't they? The entire industry is geared towards helping the wedding couple spend more than they (or you) can afford. You'll find planners plump with to-do lists that define who should do what, when, and how. Read this info, but remember that it's merely a guide, not an edict. Bridal magazines are a good source for viewing gowns but are heavy on marketing. So flip through the pages, look at the pretty pictures, glance though the articles—some are helpful—and then set them aside. One valuable resource, and it's not a magazine, is *Emily Post's Wedding Etiquette.*[5]

Your son or daughter may think to check out the web before you do, but don't be computer-shy. The wealth of vital information you'll find on line will save you unnecessary steps and simplify communication with potential wedding service vendors—reception sites, florists, photographers. Many of these sites offer free goodies, such as wedding guides, tips on budgeting, and links to such needs as an official bride name-change kit. Often couples set up their own website, which enables them to keep family and friends updated and offers helpful links to gift registries, and more.

Once you've looked over the preliminary planning resources, you may feel inundated. Take a deep breath and urge the bride and groom to get going on the important things.

- *Decide on the type of wedding they want.*
- *Make up a preliminary guest list.*
- *Create a realistic budget.*
- *Settle on a date and time for the ceremony and reception.*
- *Decide on the locations for the ceremony and reception.*
- *Assure the availability of both an officiant for the ceremony and the site for the reception.*

The month or so following the engagement is as busy and as aggravating as the month preceding the wedding day. All the family and financial issues surface and seem to need attention at once. The kids try to pick a date, but they can't confirm it until they have settled on a location for the reception and the ceremony. The date and location are often interdependent, and unless you have an approximate head count, you can't even begin to look at locations. A tiny wedding certainly doesn't warrant renting a banquet hall and, certainly, 300 people won't fit into a small chapel.

Where will the wedding be held? Will it be traditional or non-traditional, formal or casual? Is the event going to be intimate, just the family and a few close friends, or will the world be invited to share this day? These decisions define the married couple and what is important to them. It is up to the bride and groom to set the tone of their wedding, to surround themselves with whom and what they love.

What's their style?

As parents, we continue to look out for our children, so don't be surprised if you are disappointed in the kind of wedding your couple wants. If such is the case, ask yourself if you've become inflexible in your ways. Are you looking for the white wedding gown, symbolizing purity? (We'd all like to believe our children are virginal when they marry.) A religious ceremony with a dozen gowned attendants? A sit-down dinner reception with a head table? A tiered wedding cake, with the bride tossing a bouquet? A leather-bound album with posed photos?

We may want the traditional wedding regalia for our children, but we also want it for ourselves. Marriage is a rite of passage and should be celebrated with respect and dignity, shouldn't it? Let's hope so. But think again. Even if, as parents, we are paying the bill, who are we to force our couple into "clothes" that don't suit them—a wedding that's not their style?

Approach this wedding with an open mind. Should the bride and groom decide to do something unusual, like get married atop the Empire State Building and have their reception at a hot dog stand in Central Park, just go, smile and take pictures, and breathe a sigh of relief that you saved a bundle.

Do you worry more about what your friends and relatives will think than you should? If your son or daughter settles on the type of wedding you know will cause certain invited guests to whisper, keep sight of what's important. After all, whose wedding is it, anyway? Instead of trying to change your children's plans to please difficult people, consider striking the might-be-offended folks' names from the invitation list. You can always entertain them at a second, more traditional, reception—one that you arrange.

Every area of the country, urban or rural, has its own wedding style; be grateful that in today's world they've ruled out some of the more barbaric tribal rites, like sequestering the bride in a virgin's shed and having the entire tribe witness the consummation of the marriage.[6] Some of our traditions may seem just as weird to others.

A quiet ceremony followed by a dinner at a favorite restaurant or at the bride's home can be a beautiful way to begin a life. If more couples chose this route, the bridal industry would be in the poorhouse, though. Unfortunately, few couples can resist the hype that goes into getting married—the massive advertising and the focus on "doing it up big"—and that's a crying shame. All the way to the bank.

Now, I don't know how they put on weddings in your area of the country, but where I live in Connecticut, guests—especially of the senior-citizen generation—expect a big fancy dinner. There are more choices today for wedding styles than ever. The more formal ones run the gamut from postwedding brunches to evening cocktail parties. I have always envied families who could get away with a simple reception or a celebratory picnic in a park or backyard. What fun—and *cheap*, too. We do have informal weddings here in Connecticut, but they are not the norm.

23

A short "punch and cookie style" reception, although practical, can be a letdown when the wedding ceremony is formal enough to involve costly dresses for the bride and her party and tux rentals for the men. If you are a guest, you will need to give a gift and might even purchase a new outfit for the occasion.

In college, I was asked to be a bridesmaid in a friend's wedding. We sewed our own dresses out of burgundy velvet—the real silk type that crushes when you sit on it. I lived through months of planning for this big out-of-town event. As a bridesmaid, I never received an actual invitation so I had made assumptions based on weddings I had attended at home. The church was full; the ceremony, elaborate; the reception, a bomb. After the ceremony everyone went downstairs into the church hall to greet the bride and groom through a reception line. Refreshments consisted of a bowl of non-alcoholic punch and plates of bakery cookies. After an hour or so, the party broke up. The bride, groom, and everyone else left. I was perplexed. Where were we going next? *Must be to the bride's parents'*, I thought, *for the real reception*. I got into my car and raced over to their house. No one. The wedding was over. I drove home, wondering what all the fuss had been about.

At home or elsewhere?

The location of the wedding often deems its degree of formality, and perhaps its theme. An at-home wedding is apt to be less formal unless the bride lives in a mansion or on a fancy estate. By less formal, I don't mean less elegant. Formality is usually determined by the opulence of the décor and surroundings and often requires long gowns for women and dark suits or tuxedos for men. An evening wedding tends to be more formal than daytime affairs.

If the blissful couple wants to be married in your home, think hard about it. Can you keep your house company-clean while helping a bride and several bridesmaids dress for a wedding? My house looked a disaster by the time we hustled the female portion of the wedding party off to the ceremony. There were half-empty juice glasses and paper plates with smears of jam and bagel crumbs covering my tabletops and counters. Hairdryers, left-open makeup cases, and stray hairs decorated my bathrooms. I shudder at the thought of bringing guests home to such a mess. One solution is to hire a housekeeper to come in to clean up while you are at the ceremony.

Will you need to build an addition onto your home to accommodate the number of people who will attend? The general rule for row seating for a ceremony is to allow six to ten square feet of floor space per guest.[7] If space will be tight, it might make sense to rent out a place for the day.

And what about the bathroom situation? Will your plumbing system handle the number of guests you intend to entertain? A stopped-up toilet or two can really put a damper on a wedding. You can rent luxury port-o-lets, though. If they require power to operate, be sure your house electrical system can accommodate them without blowing all the circuits in your home. This happened to a friend expecting over one hundred guests. Had the problem not been quickly resolved, it would've been a nasty day for all. If you decorate port-o-lets with flowers, people who are desperate enough may even use them.

Despite potential drawbacks, an at-home wedding has an old-fashioned charm, as well as several benefits. The time saved racing around interviewing banquet hall managers can be spent on plans to redecorate. If your guest list is expansive, consider having the event catered. A friend painted, papered, and spiffed up her entire home for her daughter's wedding, down to a brand-new family room and deck. They didn't save any money, but the investment was something they could enjoy for a long time. Also, guests who are familiar with your home won't be sidetracked, following intricate directions to a reception hall.

Considerations for an at-home wedding, shower, or other event

- Do you have the indoor and outdoor space needed?
- Do you have sufficient toilet facilities to accommodate your guests?
- Does your yard need tending?
- Can your neighborhood accommodate parking?
- Will your party disturb your neighbors?
- Will your officiant be willing to conduct the ceremony outside of your place of worship?
- What items will you need to rent? A tent? Table linens?
- Will you need to hire outside help for cleaning, catering?
- Are there nearby hotels for out-of-town guests?
- Do you have enough Ibuprofen to carry you through the day?[8]

Backyard or outdoor weddings

We think of an outdoor wedding as informal, but this isn't necessarily so. I've been to several such events that were quite classy. The problem with an outdoor wedding is it can turn into a muddy disaster, should it rain. If this is your plan, be sure to either rent a canopy or indicate a rain date on your invitation. I've had my satin shoes ruined while plodding around under such a tent with a glass of champagne, wishing I'd brought a jacket. It's always cooler when it's raining. Women's dress clothes are not warm, but men wear toasty tuxedos and jackets. If your partner's jacket matches your dress, you're home free. If the wedding is held in the backyard of your home, know that guests will find excuses to go indoors and track in mud, grass, and whatnot on their shoes, even if you've provided spiffy outdoor toilet facilities.

One casual wedding I attended had a lovely garden reception with a harpist. The bride and groom barbecued the meal themselves. (They obviously did a good deal of preplanning and preparation to pull the meal off smoothly.) After the church ceremony, we were instructed to change into casual clothes for a baseball game and potato sack races. What a delightful day. The weather even cooperated, which was a Godsend, because the couple hadn't arranged for cover.

Non-traditional weddings

Many couples today defy tradition in favor of a wedding style that better suits them. It sounds romantic to get married on a boat and sail away to your honeymoon, or to be wed atop a mountain silhouetted against the sky reciting poetry to each other. The younger crowd will love it, but your staid old relatives and friends will feel cheated out a sit-down dinner with a band or DJ.

Theme weddings

If your couple dares to be different, they may want to try for a theme wedding. They are all the rage today. Some of the most memorable theme weddings are those that have meaning to the couple, not just a funky idea drawn from a hat. The theme might be centered on the location where the marriage was proposed—a garden, for example. Maybe it relates to a hobby the couple shares, such as sailing, golfing, or hiking. I've read about a wedding done with a Cinderella theme, and others worked around a New Year's Eve party and a children's party. These lend themselves to creativity and might have possibilities.

Whatever the choice, as long as it's done in good taste, the affair can be fun for everyone and, certainly, a wedding to remember.

One way to help instill common sense in a couple who is hell-bent on a wedding theme so outrageous that it ridicules the sanctity of the rite is to ask how they'd feel sharing the photos with their future children. Remind the couple this is a wedding, not a spectacle. We talked about doing a Halloween theme at my daughter's October 29th wedding, providing guests with masks and having pumpkin centerpieces and candy corn favors. Heck, we could've set a few gravestones by the entry and festooned the hall with cobwebs and rubber spiders. Then, we all laughed at the idea—and I said a silent prayer of thanks.

Destination weddings

If the wedding is intimate, the bride and groom may wish to take off to an exotic vacation spot, like Hawaii or even Paris, with their wedding party and a few close relatives and friends. The bridal industry refers to this as a "destination wedding." The nice thing about this type of wedding is everyone gets to go on the honeymoon. The downside is it is limited to those who can afford the expense of the trip, get time off from jobs, or find a reliable baby-sitter for their offspring.

Believe it or not, the trend toward destination weddings has grown for economic reasons. Given the high cost of a traditional wedding with all the trimmings, some couples feel their monies would be better spent coupling their ceremony with a resort vacation. At beach weddings, attire is bathing-suit casual and barefoot. I couldn't make my nephew's wedding in Maui, but I lusted over the photos of everyone frolicking in the island's turquoise waters.

If your couple decides on this plan, warn them about showing up at a hotel or resort to perform a wedding service without first having cleared things with the management. Famous spots may require you to purchase their package. I know of a couple who tried to get married at Disney World and were stopped as the ceremony was about to be performed. To complete the ceremony, they diverted the interfering security guard by sending him on an information errand. That's no way to start a life.

If your son or daughter wants to be married in some faraway spot, suggest he or she ally with a travel agent or wedding consultant[9] who specializes in destination weddings. This will assure everything is "cool" with the management of the facility they will use; that they will know about and be prepared to fulfill the necessary legal requirements for marriage—blood tests, licenses—in that country, state, city, or village; and that an officiant, as well as all vendor services needed will be there at the right time.

Surprise weddings

At a surprise wedding, anyone can be the surprised—the guests, the bride, or the parents. This is typically a regular wedding, complete with ceremony and reception, not an elopement. The spontaneity of such an event only adds to the emotion of a wedding. I guarantee, no matter how it happens, if you witness such an event you will sob with joy. I heard of a wedding where the prospective groom invited the unknowing bride-to-be to a "party." He produced a justice of the peace, a wedding party, and a gown. I was not privy to the details, but I certainly hope the groom thought to procure a marriage license and had the necessary blood tests taken care of beforehand.

Nail down the when and how

An engaged couple usually has some idea of how soon they plan to wed—in a year or two, six months, or next week! A one-year planning window is common; but depending on their circumstances, they may decide to get married later on. Without the ever-present threat of pregnancy, due to the advent of reliable birth control, there seems to be little reason to rush into marriage. Many wait until they are older and settled in their jobs, instead of plunging into wedded bliss right after high school or college. Today's couples are more money conscious than we used to be. They are smart enough to walk into marriage with their eyes open and a clear head. Their reasons are sound: building a life together, creating a steady home environment to raise children, and choosing a caring partner they can live with for many years.

Not necessarily a June bride

The most popular seasons for weddings are spring, summer, and fall. It may interest you to know that, in olden times, spring was a time of orgies, so most women shunned getting married then. Over time, this old wives' tale translated into spring being a time for fertility, new birth. June became popular for weddings when it was the norm for young women to marry right after graduation from high school or college. I was married in early July for that reason.

Today, young folks choose to marry during a particular season because the timing fits their work schedules or, simply, because they love it. A winter wedding lends itself to lush velvets and shades of greens. With an off-season wedding in the winter months, there is a greater choice of reception facilities and photographers. Other service providers' schedules are more open and rates are usually lower. At a January wedding I attended, the bride was seasonally radiant in a white, fur-trimmed satin gown, complete with matching fur headpiece, and carried red roses. Lovely. One exception might be a destination wedding held in a tropical area, where our winter may be their high season.

In the Northeast, fall has become an even more popular wedding time than spring. A backdrop of brilliant foliage in still comfortable, "no-coat" weather is appealing and outdoor photographs, spectacular. Fall and winter weddings lend themselves to navy blues, blacks, and deep burgundies. In cooler weather, we want to be inside and cozy. The day is shorter, so the grounds of a reception facility are less important.

Spring and summer make us think of peaches and sage greens and daisies in straw baskets. I envision a summer wedding as less formal, an afternoon frolic on a large lawn with lemonade and champagne. Reception guests can mingle outdoors well into the night.

If you plan around a major holiday, such Christmas or New Year's, it's possible to save on decorations and flowers, as the facility will be already attired in holiday garb. People traveling from afar are more apt to attend a wedding held over a long weekend, such as Memorial Day, Labor Day, New Year's, or Thanksgiving because they will need to take less time off from jobs. However, traffic may be horrendous and airfares and hotels rates will be upped.

Set the date and time

The first hurdle is to coordinate the date and time for the wedding. In the early stages, before deposits are made and contracts are signed, the wedding date is not cast in cement. It can't be. With only fifty-two weekends in a year, many couples vie for the same great facilities and vendors. If your couple has their heart set on a particular date, they may be disappointed to find their church is booked, that there's a waiting list for the wedding site they chose, and that their favored photographer's schedule is bulging. If this will be a religious ceremony and premarital counseling is required, your couple will need to allow extra time—six months, perhaps—to complete this obligation before the ceremony.

But what if your couple has arranged for a particular date, only to find it conflicts with other occasions? Does their wedding day land on a religious holiday, such as Good Friday, where Lenten restrictions are in place, or on a Jewish holiday that limits travel and may involve fasting? Is this the anniversary of Grandma's death? For some, getting married on the date something dreadful happened, such as September 11, is a bad omen. Yet, an optimist may consider it as replacing a sad memory with a happy one. Help your couple work through any dilemmas and make the decision that's right for them while there is still the flexibility to move the wedding date to a different weekend or day of the week.

If the wedding is guided by religious affiliation, timing can be an issue. In the Jewish religion, weddings can't be held on the Sabbath, which is Friday sundown thru Saturday. When I was married, Catholic nuptial masses were performed before noon on a Saturday, which meant a lunchtime reception (and no breakfast for those receiving communion). Times change. Some of these restrictions may have eased by now.

The evening wedding is particularly popular. The attire is more formal and guests have a chance to dress up in formal wear. At a five o'clock wedding, for example, the reception usually begins about seven, and dancing goes on until midnight. This creates another problem. Guests traveling long distances won't want to (and shouldn't) drive home late at night, so it's important to make certain there are accommodations available near-by. At my second daughter's wedding we had a lovely late afternoon candlelight service we would've felt foolish performing earlier in the day. Another nice thing about an evening wedding is that the wedding party has all day to run errands and fuss with hair-dos and attire. In our family, the men like to play a round of golf the day of the ceremony.

Information management

Once we got going on researching ceremonies and wedding sites and all the trappings, it wasn't long before I had accumulated a sizable pile of data: lists of reception halls to explore with my children, torn-out pages from bridal magazines touting etiquette rules, and copies of paperwork detailing our forthcoming event. My daughter started with a simple fill-in-the-blanks planning guide, and then graduated to a loose-leaf notebook with tabs as her information expanded. A canvas tote held her book, as well a plethora of bridal magazines with dog-eared pages marking the bridal gown and bridesmaid ideas. This bag traveled with her everywhere (and now resides in my closet).

As mother of the bride, I didn't need that much paraphernalia, but I did have to devise a way to organize the information I needed to manage the activities I was responsible for. I divided proposals, payment receipts, and contracts into manila folders by event or vendor and stored these near the kitchen phone. If you are the mother of the groom, you'll want to keep information handy for gift registries and lists of potential hotels that attending friends and relatives might need. You'll likely need a file for the rehearsal dinner and possibly the stag party.

I exchanged details with my daughter and her attendants via phone calls and e-mail. We also kept shared spreadsheet listings of the guest list, which detailed addresses, phone numbers, e-mail addresses, and attendance and meal choice data. E-mail makes this a snap to keep updated. Before long, you'll find you have several spreadsheets going. If you are the mother of the bride, in addition to the guest list sheet, you will have a personal sheet for the bridal shower, as well as any other parties you are involved with.

If you are paying for much of the wedding, you'll definitely want to keep a cost spreadsheet to stay on track with expected costs and payment due dates. We'll get to money management soon. A mother of the groom who is not heavily involved in planning the reception will likely want a guest spreadsheet for the rehearsal dinner and perhaps the stag. Needless to say, such spreadsheets can be created on computer in a program like Excel, or written by hand on lined paper. You might check the web for programs to track all facets of wedding planning.

Keep File Folders Handy

1. Reception information: menus, dinner info, guest lists, seating plan
2. Vendor contracts for all vendors, and copies of checks and confirmation letters
3. Registry information for gifts
4. Bridal shower information: directions, menus, guest lists, listing of local bed and breakfasts and hotels for overnight guests
5. Rehearsal Dinner guest list, restaurant paperwork, and seating plan
6. Attire information: locations of bridal and tux shop, phone numbers, and receipts

If you are computer savvy, you might carry such information on your cell phone, iPad, or computer. At home, you might find it easier and faster to reference good old hard copy.

Should you consider a wedding planning service?

It never hurts to investigate the idea, especially if time is dear to you or the bride and neither of you feels comfortable taking on the brunt of planning a large, formal wedding. While the movie *Father of the Bride* offers viewers a slanted vision of the wedding consultant industry, it underscores the fact that someone you pay is responsible for handling all the details and making certain the wedding comes off flawlessly. Wedding planners' rates vary according to their expertise and the size and scope of the wedding. An efficient, experienced coordinator should be able to pass along enough savings to cover his or her fee, according to the buzz advertising their services.[10]

You can commission a planner or coordinator at several levels:

1. A full service wedding planner handles everything, beginning to end, which includes creating, organizing, and managing timelines

and taking responsibility for all vendor activity. Their fees range between 10% and 20% of the total wedding budget.

2. Coordinators and consultants help you to organize budgets, schedules, and timelines and will *advise you* on ways to save money and avoid problems. They typically charge between 5% and 15% of the total wedding budget.

3. Day of Wedding planners ensure the events occurring on the wedding day go smoothly by creating timelines, confirming vendors and coordinating details. Their flat fee is between $500 and $2000.

4. Wedding directors, possibly provided by the ceremony site, ensure church or synagogue rules are followed.

It is difficult to plan a destination wedding unless you work with a wedding planner who specializes in that area. Call the city's tourist office for a referral or contact the Association of Bridal Consultants. As with any financial decision, it's in your best interest to check out references and to use only reputable consultants—someone who does it for a living, not as a sideline.

As with any other vendor you hire, use caution.

- Are they accessible? Do they return phone calls or e-mails?
- Are they getting kickbacks for recommending certain vendors?
- Is their taste and style compatible with yours?
- Do you have a clear contract that details their duties, costs, and expenses?
- What happens if you are not happy with their work?

Awk. They eloped!

It happens. The couple gets fed up with waiting and skips out on us. The next thing we know, they appear at our door with big grins or call, e-mail, or text us with the happy announcement. If you haven't already invested time and money in a wedding, you might be thrilled. Think of all the money saved. Now, they can afford to buy a condo or even a house. Or you might be stunned and depressed. You missed out on sharing their glory.

Not to worry. You may end up with a full-blown wedding after all. Since the ceremony was likely perfumed by a justice of the peace, the couple may want to repeat the ceremony in their own church. Friends and family at home will naturally attend, and afterwards you will have to celebrate. Even without a second ceremony, friends and family will be itching to congratulate the couple, which spells, p-a-r-t-y.

Dear Joy,

I'd heard weddings cost a bundle, but this is ridiculous!

CHAPTER 5

Survive Sticker Shock

"WE JUST WANT AN INTIMATE little gathering—only our immediate family and closest friends," they tell you. You nod happily in agreement, thinking about all the money you are going to save. If your couple is planning to pay for their own wedding, you'll save even more. Your husband, practical man that he is, has been trying to convince them to elope. He's even offered to buy the ladder and, with the savings, give them enough money for a down payment on a home. Your prospective son-in-law considers the suggestion and then discards it. Your daughter is whining for a real wedding, and he loves her too much to have her do without. Besides, he really wants it too.

Your children have attended a wagonload of weddings for their friends over the past year or two. They have stood up as groomsmen, bridesmaids, and maids of honor too many times. They know the ropes now, how it is supposed to be, and they want it all—the gown, the flowers the parties, and the presents. I can't say I blame them. Having a big wedding is like reigning as prince and princess for the day as guests of honor at a party, especially if it's given by the king and queen, dear old Mom and Dad.

Weddings are seldom practical. You start out building a small hut and end up with a castle. "Sticker shock" is the trauma of realizing how much this wedding is liable to cost. The average cost of a wedding has increased from $15,200 in 1990 to $26,500 in 2010.[11]

The amount of promotional marketing done for a wedding is astounding. Bridal magazines, shows, and shops are full of information about what every bride "must" do or buy to have the "perfect" wedding. And of course, who doesn't want a perfect wedding? It starts by softening the bride and groom up for the kill by convincing them they need an expensive diamond. They must select a dinnerware pattern—the finest china, the most exotic flatware. And crystal glasses—they simply cannot entertain without these delicate, breakable delights.

By the time wedding planning rolls around, it's no wonder your child wants it all. She's been preprogrammed that if she doesn't have a designer gown, wear real pearls, serve a sit-down prime rib dinner to her guests, and decorate with oodles of flowers, her wedding won't be special. You and I already know this is nonsense. But how do we convince her that materialistic things don't make a wedding special? It's the glow of happiness on her face as she glides toward her intended. Guests can get drunk just watching two people in love dance. A wedding is magical. It doesn't require a fancy ballroom, and she doesn't even need an expensive dress. The two most important elements for the wedding are there, with or without the expense. Two people in love. What more do we need?

My daughter didn't buy that either.

We ended up with the big "do" and the outlay that went along with it. The first wedding was the hardest. We argued about every expense that we didn't want to take on. Why did their friends need to invite dates? Do they really need favors? Maybe we can find a gown on sale. One hundred fifty dollars per person is too much to pay for the reception. Orchids are expensive. Why not roses? She sulked; we held our ground. It went on and on. We won some; we lost some. In the end, we found ways to compromise by deciding the cheapest way to accomplish what was important to each of us. She had the wedding she wanted, and it didn't cost us as much as it could have. The best part is we set a precedent we could manage for our next two weddings.

Show me the money

Despite who pays for what, you, the in-laws, and the to-be-wed couple are in this deal together. If the couple needs to spend money arranging for the honeymoon, they'll have less to contribute to the other wedding costs. The balancing of dollars and cents will vary from one situation to another.

Traditionally, the cost of a wedding has been the responsibility of tl. parents, a throwback from the dowry days. However, with today's costs, many of us cannot afford such an affair without going into debt. ⊃o we need to be creative.

There are many ways to slice up a wedding cake. Nowadays, it is very common for the bride and groom to pay for all or most wedding expenses themselves, or to split more evenly the wedding-related expenses between both sets of parents. Thus, it's not unusual for both sets of parents to co-host. If the groom has an extra-large family, the groom's parents may offer to pay for their half of the reception. The easiest way to handle such as situation is to ask the groom to act as intermediary and to have the couple coordinate bill payments, using contributions from both sets of parents.

> *Who Pays These Days?[12]*
> *29% Bride*
> *21% Bride's parents*
> *29% Groom*
> *14% Groom's parents*
> *07% Others*

Can your couple pay?

We usually have some sense of the financial condition of our young ones. A couple getting married right from high school or college graduation, as was once the norm, has not had the opportunity to build up a nest egg, so they may rely on their parents to fund their wedding. Many young folks today, however, are waiting until they have established themselves financially by pursuing their careers and building their savings. They have definite ideas about their wedding and are willing and able to pay for it themselves in order to get exactly what they wish.

If the betrothed are taking care of everything, or mostly everything, you may still be consulted on expense management. However, understand that you can chime in righteously on any expense that you have committed to take on; otherwise, you are simply an advisor. But, you have gained the luxury of splurging! Offer to buy your daughter an outrageously expensive gown.

Give the to-be-wed couple their honeymoon or the down payment for a new home.

Money management

If you've begun some preliminary investigation, you've already experienced the first shock, the horrendous cost of putting on a wedding. Help control the amount and allocation of expenses by putting together a budget you collectively can live with. There are many resources available on line and in wedding planning guides to help you do this, so I'll just give you a working base.

Regardless of who pays for what, *someone* has to take on the responsibility of the costs, whether it's you as the parents of the bride or the couple themselves. Whoever is doing this will find it easier to manage the monies if the wedding costs are kept separate from routine expenses—rent, car payments, and fitness center dues. Do this by opening a separate checking account. Deposit funds for payment into this account, and then draw from them to pay wedding-related bills. In addition, you may settle on using a particular credit card for large deposits and payments. This will allow you extra time to pay off the sum (do be sure to pay on time so as not to accrue interest), and if you've selected a card that allows you to accumulate travel miles, you'll have a bonus as well.

When monies are going to be contributed by several people, there are two ways to handle such a situation. Once you have estimated total expense, collect the portion these people have agreed to pay in a lump sum for deposit into the wedding account. If someone offers to pay for a specific service—the photographer or the flowers, for example—he or she might prefer to be billed directly. In this case, simply turn over the handling of that facet of the wedding to the person paying for it.

Create an affordable budget

Wait! Before you sign on the dotted line, sit down and figure out how much money you (and anyone else who is sharing the expenses) can afford to contribute towards this wedding. If necessary, speak with your financial planner or accountant to help put the money outlay in line with your routine expenses. This may eliminate the need to take out a second mortgage on your home, give up your beach house, or sell your convertible.

One set of bridal parents offered $7,000 as their contribution, leaving the engaged couple with the option of working within their parents' budget or adding money from their own savings to cover additional costs. The actual cost of that wedding was $10,000, but that was many years ago. We used this figure as a guideline for our first wedding and, although we ended up spending much more, it helped us keep things under control during the planning stages.

To avoid having a heart attack when the bills roll in, my advice is to keep two budgets: the one you will pay, and the one you tell your children you will pay. Planning a wedding is like building a house. We start with a firm budget with every intention of sticking to it, but as the event unfolds, we begin to relax and then indulge on little extras, like brass faucets instead of chrome or tiled floors in lieu of linoleum. This is normal, so mentally pad the budget you've drawn up for your couple with a few thousand dollars extra for splurges. For example, the overall cost of our "$10,000" wedding was $15,000 because we agreed to buy our daughter a designer wedding gown, and paid extra for calla lilies to give our wedding the elegance we wanted.

Plan a Budget

1. Decide what you can afford.
2. Determine your expenses.
3. Prioritize expenses.
4. Set limits.

Research

Begin planning your wedding budget by getting a handle on the costs of key expenses. Ask your daughter to talk to recently-married friends and pump them for information and ideas. Contact vendors who interest you and ask for estimates. (This is a collective "you" that includes the bride, groom, and their parents.) What do photographers and videographers cost these days? How about flowers, including table centerpieces? And don't forget music.

You'll need it for the ceremony as well as for the reception. By the way, the ceremony isn't free either.

Once you've collected some facts, you will be able to estimate realistically the amount to allot to each area of the budget.

Average Wedding Costs Breakdown[13]

Wedding Reception 45-55%
Ceremony 2%
Wedding Attire 10%
Flowers and Décor 5-10%
Photos and Video 8-12%
Music 4-6%
Transportation 2%
Wedding Rings 2-5%
Invitations 2-4%
Taxes and Tips 5-8%
Misc. Unexpected Costs 10%

Make up a chart similar to the one provided in this chapter, or go on line and take advantage of the many wedding budget planning resources. To hone in on estimates for your area of the country, tap into *Real Simple's* e-zine.[14] The final tally of the estimated costs column will be your budget. The budget for a simple wedding should include items you cannot provide yourself but intend to purchase, as well as the cost of tasks you plan to do on your own with the help of friends or family.

This sample worksheet includes the majority of expenses you might incur. Leave some extra lines on your spreadsheet to include unanticipated expenses.

Wedding Budget Worksheet

Basic Expense	Budgeted Cost	Actual Cost
Wedding Reception: Site fee (if applicable) Catering costs Bar & beverages Wedding cake Favors Valet parking Transportation		
Photos & Videos: Photographer Videographer Engagement portrait Wedding album package		
Flowers & Décor: Ceremony-site flowers Bridal bouquet Wedding party flowers Reception centerpieces Corsages/boutonnieres		
Music: Ceremony Cocktail hour Reception		
Wedding Attire: Bride's dress Headpiece/veil Lingerie Shoes/wrap Hair & makeup Groom's ensemble		
Stationary: Invitations and enclosures Announcements Thank-you notes Postage Ceremony programs		
Parties: Bridal Shower Stag Rehearsal Dinner Hospitality room After-party Day-after brunch		
Extras: Bridal luncheon Attendant gifts Wedding rings Marriage license Church/Synagogue fees Officiant fees Assistant fees Wedding Insurance Taxes and tips		
	Grand Total=	**Grand Total=**

Once you have completed your primal scream, settle down to business and work with your son or daughter and his or her intended to help them create the wedding they want without going into hock for the rest of your collective lives. Decide which events you and your husband will pay for, and then add some bucks to handle them into your special parent's budget.

Now that you have made up a list of expected expenses and estimated costs, go through it and check off the expenses that are absolutes—the officiant's fee, for example. Total up the estimate of absolute or fixed costs and subtract this from the number you have collectively arrived at as your wedding budget. Subtract this from your total of available funds. This is the amount you have left to work with for variable costs, such as flowers, limos, and the reception.

> Money available $15,000
> Total fixed costs—3,000
> Money to spend on remaining items $12,000

Prioritize expenses

The key players in the planning—the bride, groom, and their parents—will have specific ideas as to how the available money should be allocated. These will undoubtedly come out in discussions. If not, ask some questions. While the bride may focus on having the ultimate wedding gown, parents may be more concerned about "putting on the Ritz" at the reception, and the groom may wish to elope to avoid the whole expense. Understanding priorities helps with determining how the various portions of the budget should be allocated; i.e., is everyone in agreement that 80 percent of the monies be spent on the reception?

Divide and conquer

Now, take a deep breath and calm down. While the lump sum seems enormous, it will be paid in installments over the course of the wedding planning cycle, which could be a year or more. Dividing the monies due into

chunks makes the payment process more palatable. One
less painful to pay when it is divided into four payments (

The typical florist will require an initial deposit, a pa
before the wedding, with final payment one week befc
Photographers vary. Most want all but 10 percent of the tot _.. ine
wedding day. We dealt with one company that only required a small deposit
to hold a date, but would not send a photographer to the wedding unless the
balance for all the albums and pictures was paid beforehand. There was no
room to negotiate on this either.

As you commit to vendors and sign contracts, go through your calendar
and mark the dates when payments will be due for each. With the exception
of the final payments due the week of the wedding, the dates will vary. If
there's a large gap between the initial planning and the wedding date—say, ten
months, it's easy to bypass a due date. (Maybe it's a mental block.) Also, keep
track of changes. The payment amounts will need to be adjusted whenever
you add or delete items or services.

Most of us need to plan for large installments that are not part of our
routine monthly expenses. Note that as the wedding date closes in, the
installments grow larger. Those final payments are killers because they fall
due at the same time. But look at it this way: you have time to plan for the
big hit even if it means taking out a loan or robbing a bank.

Ways to save beaucoup buckaroos:

- Limit your guest list.
- Scale down the reception. An afternoon tea is cheaper than a five-course meal or a buffet dinner.
- Reduce the number of attendants to save on flowers, meals, and thank-you gifts.
- Avoid unexpected costs by reviewing contracts to verify items included.
- Choose an off-season date when caterers, photographers, bands, and DJs are so hungry for gigs that they'll give you a reduced rate.
- Skimp on favors and centerpieces; most are left on the table, anyway.
- Rent accessories, such as linens, instead of buying them.

Do the easy things yourselves.
- Keep abreast of tips for savings offered by bridal guides and websites.

Avoid surprises

To keep your budgeting on track, be sure all service provider details are clearly outlined in a written contract. Avoid dealing with vendors who provide hastily scribbled or verbal estimates. Opt for those who will give you item-by-item listings and will contract for specific prices. We found better peace of mind with firm quotes. When we got estimates for calla lily arrangements, cost variables depended on whether the flowers were in season, the size of the flowers—regular or giant—and how many would be needed to make up the bouquets, table arrangements, or corsages we wanted. The florist that handed us a pencil-scribbled estimate lost the deal.

Dealing with service providers takes project coordination, tact, and intuition. Do your research before signing. If you feel squishy about the vendor, check the company's credentials with the Better Business Bureau to make sure the company isn't being chased by unhappy customers. Keep all paperwork and evidence of payment, so if things aren't right you'll have the documentation to request a refund; i.e., the cake that never arrived at the reception hall. Take the time to sample the goodies. Have a test meal prepared and served by the restaurant, reception facility, or caterer. Sample cakes and listen to a band's music or a DJ's banter before committing.

Remember . . .

- Decide what you can afford.
- Determine expenses.
- Prioritize importance.
- Get quotes and cost ranges.
- Set limits.
- A wedding doesn't need to be expensive to be beautiful.

What if?

I'm certain you have no desire to add another expense to your growing mound, but have you thought about how much money might be lost if, for some reason, the wedding is cancelled? Consider taking out wedding insurance. Learn about it on line by doing a search on "wedding insurance."

Dear Joy,

Getting everything coordinated is driving us nuts. I've been secretly praying they'd just elope.

CHAPTER 6

Ways to Say "I Do"

REGARDLESS OF ALL THE FLUFF, the heart of a wedding is the ceremony. Without the couple's vows to each other in a legal or religious presence there can be no legal marriage. Trust that your blissful duo will have specific ideas of how and where they want to take their vows.

You may or may not be asked to go with the bride and groom on their first round of site investigation, but once the couple has settled on a chapel, church, a park, or mountaintop they love, you may want to visit the site to be sure it will work. This is especially true in the case of a theme wedding. Is there enough space to accommodate all of the wedding guests? Will you need to rent a canopy, chairs, or any extraneous gear to make the site comfortable for the ceremony? Will this place be available on the date and time needed? Are there any permissions required to conduct a wedding there?

If the chosen location is a church or synagogue, speak with an on-premise priest, rector, pastor, or rabbi to set things in motion. Ask about the expected length of the ceremony. If a high mass or special service is included, a ceremony can run as long as ninety minutes. You'll need this information if you will be hosting a reception at a separate location. As you get further along in your planning, you will want more detailed information, but this is enough to get started.

Suppose the choice ceremony site is an out-of-town or out-of-country location? Laws vary city-to-city, state-to-state, and country-to-country. For a wedding here in the U.S.A., your couple will need to call or stop in at the

County Clerk's Office of the Registrar in that town to learn what is required before the marriage can take place. Your couple may encounter unexpected restrictions. Some states require couples to register in person or in the same state or country where the ceremony will be performed. Is there a waiting period? Some states require up to sixty days. Will they need witnesses? Blood tests? Proof of age?

Be particularly vigilant when dealing with a foreign country, like Greece, Paris, or the British Virgin Islands. (Remember that Alaska, Hawaii, and Puerto Rico, and the Virgin Islands are United States territories.) I strongly advise that the to-be-wed-duo work with a travel agent or consultant who has had experience setting up weddings in that particular country. The couple needs to know all the requirements to avoid a catastrophe at the eleventh hour.

Understand that, although there will be variances from location to location, there will always be restrictions concerning age, marrying of relatives and, possibly, marrying persons of the same gender. If your son or daughter has been married before, a copy of the divorce degree, death certificate or annulment may be needed to obtain a license to rewed. In a religious ceremony, the couple may need to obtain special permission from the church or synagogue. As examples: divorce is not recognized by the Catholic church if the ex-spouse is still living, so annulment papers would need to be produced or procured; in the Episcopal church, the couple must seek special dispensation from the area bishop to wed; and, in the Jewish faith, a divorced woman cannot remarry without an official rabbinical document of divorce.

If your son or daughter's love is not a United States citizen, the couple should contact the Office of the Immigration and Nationalization Service, U.S. embassies and consulates abroad, or the U.S. Department of State Visa Office for information about obtaining a visa and to learn the specifics about any documents necessary for the wedding to go forward.

Who will do the honors?

There are many choices as far as an officiant is concerned. Will this be a civil ceremony or a religious ceremony? Many couples who are not particularly religious choose to be married in a civil ceremony by a justice of the peace. One advantage of a civil ceremony is that the ceremony and reception can be held in one place. Traveling is simplified, and guests won't be waylaid between the church and reception.

This may also be the case with a wedding held outdoors—the exception being Jewish ceremonies, which are commonly held outdoors under a *chuppah*, a wedding tent symbolic of their faith. With a destination wedding, regardless of religion, it may be easiest to marry in a civil ceremony and then have a second, religious ceremony performed once on home ground.

Officiants qualified to preside over a civil ceremony:

- Mayor of a city or village
- City clerk or a deputy of a city of over one million people
- Marriage officer appointed by a town or village board
- Justice or judge in most courts
- Village, town, or county justice
- Court clerk who has legal authority to perform marriages
- Person who has been given temporary authority by a judge or clerk

Aside from the convenience, we parents normally like to see our children married with the blessings of both God and State. Religious ceremonies can be performed by any member of the clergy who has been officially ordained and granted authority to perform marriage ceremonies from a governing church body, or one who has been chosen by a spiritual group to preside over their affairs. In the case of a Native American wedding, a tribal chief can do the honors.

If the couple is of the same religion, getting the ceremony arranged in either of their parishes or synagogues will be fairly easy, as they will be already in sync with the laws and restrictions of that church or synagogue.

The snags in our grand plan occur when we vary from the norm.

Suppose the bride and groom want a favorite uncle, Father Joe, to perform the ceremony in lieu of the host priest? They would need to obtain permission, of course, and also find out what, if any, other documentation the officiant needs to provide. Do they need proof that Uncle Joe is a bona fide priest?

In an interfaith marriage, the couple may use two officiants, each representing the particular faiths of the bride and groom, or hold two separate ceremonies. Of course, the church or synagogue would need to approve any arrangements. There may be restrictions about performing the rite at the altar or including the vows in the traditional nuptial mass. Having two separate ceremonies can become complicated. Should guests be invited to both ceremonies, or should the ceremonies be private? Two receptions? Ouch, that hurts.

Religions where marriage is considered a sacrament—Roman Catholic, Jewish, and Episcopal—have strict laws regarding interfaith marriages. Should your son or daughter choose to marry outside the family religion, the partner will need to agree to certain things. These vary. If the bride is Catholic and the groom is Baptist, say, the bride's church may require the groom to sign an agreement to raise the couple's children as Catholics. These situations can become thorny if the non-Catholic partner is inflexible—or belongs to a strict religion, such as the Jewish faith.

Unless your family is strong in a particular religion, you shouldn't expect that your child will hold to it. Religious affiliation is ultimately the decision of the bride and groom. It's possible you have influence here, but don't be a pushy about the subject or you may lose. My experience is that when to-be-wed couples are raised in differing religions, those with the strongest beliefs are likely to prevail.

As a divorcee', I was excommunicated from the Catholic Church, so my children's religious training was interrupted. They were not full-fledged anything, leaving them vulnerable. My first daughter married a strong Catholic, after completing her religious education, and will be Catholic ever after. My second daughter fell in love with a Methodist fellow, and they began attending church together. Then I knew the relationship had become serious. They exchanged vows in an exquisite candlelight ceremony at the Simsbury Methodist church, one of few churches in Connecticut with a bell tower. We hired a carillonneur and ended our ceremony with the peal of bells.

My son's true love, on the other hand, hadn't been baptized, which meant she was non-Christian. There was a time when allowing children to select their own religions, once they grew up, was in vogue. This surfaced as an issue when our parish minister refused to perform the ceremony. So it was civil ceremony or find a religion and get baptized quickly. I was fortunate my son and his fiancée' took my advice and spoke with the minister at our church, a wonderful Santa-type fellow, about how they might proceed. When they decided to move forward on a church ceremony, I was both delighted and relieved (I had been plagued with guilt for years). She was baptized, and my son was confirmed in our faith. When the two of them walked down the aisle on their wedding day, their union blessed, it brought me to tears. It's comforting to know that all my grandchildren, unlike my own children, will have a solid, religious upbringing.

Another situation that can occur when the couple is to be married in an area where neither of them or their families reside is finding a church of their denomination to perform the ceremony. When my first daughter and her fiancé sought out a Catholic church in our home town, they had trouble securing a date because preference was given to parishioners. Eventually, they located a kind priest in Mystic, where the reception was to be held, who was happy to oblige them. Everything went off without a hitch—or should I say, *with* a hitch.

Honor thy family

It's tempting to exercise whatever parental influence we still have to encourage our children to marry within our faith or nationality. Years ago, when the world was smaller, parents had more to say about a daughter's wedding partner. A Jewish girl I knew in my college days cried her eyes out for days; she had to breakup with her boyfriend because he wasn't Jewish. I'm Italian, and I can remember my dad saying, "Why can't you find a nice Italian boy"? In old Italian families, the parents made the match. Antiquated as this may seem, fix-ups by parents are still part of certain nationalities. Marriage is difficult enough when you love someone.

Each of us is steeped in ways of our culture, whether we realize it or not. We were born and raised in it and surrounded by it. It affects the way we dress, act, and eat, and you can bet that all the relatives of both bride and groom will have certain expectations about the honoring of traditions. I know you hope, as I did, that your son or daughter will hold true to certain customs. Not for worry about what the relatives will think, but because you know they will ground your child, give him or her the right start on a new family.

> *In many African-American weddings, jumping over a broom is a symbol of sweeping away the old and welcoming the new. This practice comes from an old African tribal ritual of placing sticks on the ground to represent the couple's new home. Today, "jumping the broom" symbolizes the newlyweds' connection to each other and their heritage.*[15]

Mixed marriages, with partners of differing religions and/or nationalities, are more prevalent today, as they should be. I'm still waiting for all faiths and cultures to merge into one happy world. When it comes to a rite as serious as marriage, it is hard to cast aside our proven ways. Rent the movie *My Big Fat Greek Wedding* to get a clear view of the bonds family can impose on a couple.

In a mixed marriage of any sort, it's important to respect the traditions of both cultures, even if it means having a double ceremony or two separate receptions. At one wedding I attended, the groom's family was from Scotland. In lieu of a tuxedo, the groom met his bride at the altar wearing a kilt made of a tartan plaid that represented his family's clan. It's Scottish tradition for the groom to pass his tartan sash over to the bride as a ceremony finale. Afterwards, guests enjoyed cocktails to the wail of bagpipes.

An Irish bride I know wore her mom's wedding dress; the family crest had been embroidered on the train. She married a Jewish fellow. Both a Rabbi and a Catholic priest shared the ceremony, performed at a neutral church altar. At the reception, a few Jewish traditions were worked into the festivities. Both bride and groom were hoisted up on chairs and carried around the room, and the groom stomped on a wine glass from which they had both sipped (a custom representing the fragility of love).

In accordance with state regulations, a same-sex wedding may be legally documented as a marriage or other recognized partnership, such as a civil union. If the partnership isn't legally recognized, the wedding may be a religious or symbolic ceremony attended by family and friends to publicize the couple's commitment to each other. Personally, I applaud the right of any loving couple to make a lifetime commitment. A former workmate, from whom I hadn't heard in years, called me to announce she had chosen a life partner and they had adopted an adorable baby girl from China. What courage, what conviction. I love it!

Dear Joy,

There's so much to do at once I don't know where to begin—or even if I should.

CHAPTER 7

Plan the Reception

N OT ONLY DOES A RECEPTION cost big bucks, no matter how intimate the gathering or how simple the food and drink, but the process needs to be constantly monitored to ensure it goes smoothly. While the entire wedding procedure is imbued with parties, the big finale will be the reception. We touched on various styles of weddings earlier. Now let's get specific.

Using the cost figure you arrived at for the reception from your wedding budget, and keeping in mind the type of location, style, theme of the wedding, and the time of the ceremony, decide on the kind of reception that would work best. Here are some classic options:

> *Wedding Brunch*
> *Luncheon*
> *Afternoon Tea*
> *Cocktails*
> *Cocktails with passed hors d'oeuvres and buffet stations*
> *Sit-down Dinner*
> *Elaborate Buffet Dinner*

It's not necessary to serve a meal at the reception. However, if you plan to hold the event during normal mealtime hours, 11:00 am to 1:00 pm or 5:00 pm to 8:00 pm, guests will likely arrive hungry and expectant. Also, understand that people need nutrition every three or four hours. If your reception does not include foods that are hearty enough to count as a meal, plan to have a reception lasting no more than three hours.

If you have a ton of guests on your roster and not too much money, it may be cheaper to avoid having a sit-down, soup-to-nuts dinner. A morning wedding could be followed by a brunch or a simple luncheon. How about serving afternoon tea after a ceremony held past the lunch hour? This works particularly well if children will be invited. If the wedding will be large, folks will linger longer to visit, so be sure to include something heartier than cake and cookies. At any daytime event, a celebratory toast is in order.

For a late afternoon or early evening wedding, why not follow the trend and have a cocktail party? Keep in mind that booze can cost more than (or as much as) food if yours is a drinking crowd. Serve substantial appetizers with liquor to help stave off inebriation. Passed trays of goodies and serving stations offering small bowls of pasta, salad, and sliced meats wedged in tiny rolls are popular accompaniments to cocktails. With a cocktail party, there'll be no need to fiddle with a seating plan. Folks will stand or sit wherever there is space. Without dealing with a dinner, your room will accommodate a larger crowd.

If you are offering a meal, but believe you'll save money by serving it buffet-style, rather than served and sit-down, think again. A buffet dinner or one with several serving stations is often costlier, as a greater variety of foods will be offered. When guests serve themselves, the advantage of portion control is lost. Also, more dishes, silverware, and linens are needed, as well as hired help or restaurant staff to man the stations and keep foods replenished.

Whichever reception option you choose, be sure to include dessert—the wedding cake, of course. Also, specify in the invitation the type of event this will be—i.e., cocktail and hors d'oeuvres, teas and cake, light lunch—so guests won't arrive expecting a gala meal and find themselves noshing on celery and dip. The type of reception you have decided on and the size of your guest list will be dictating factors in picking a place to hold the reception.

Where oh where should it be?

If your couple has a place in mind, it's a good start. You may already have decided to use your home for the reception. If so, your focus will be making arrangements for outside vendors needed to pull off the event and deciding whether or not you want to prepare your own food or hire a caterer. Bear in mind that no matter what type of facility you choose, you'll need to consider the comfort of your guests and the attributes of the particular site.

With a commercial location, such as a banquet hall, begin with finding out if it is available for the date and time you have in mind. But wait! Every place you call for information wants to know head count. This figure dictates the room size needed and determines whether they can accommodate you. So your couple drafts an invitation list.

This is when the first fracas occurs.

What happened to the intimacy part? Their "few friends" number fifty and, of course, they'll want to bring dates. Okay, so you are up to one hundred people and no relatives' names are listed. They didn't even count you and your family amongst the guests. An oversight, I'm sure. You pout and argue with them, struggling to make the list more complete. This is when you find out how many future cousins and uncles-in-law are on the groom's side of the family.

The first crack at the guest list needs to represent the four key parties involved: bride, groom, and both parents' lists of relatives and close friends. There may be subsets of these. One bride I know had four sets of parents to manage; each parent had remarried. This increased the guest list exponentially. Any guest list can easily get out of hand if not managed. Take a deep breath, limit the infighting, and insist everyone face the reality of the situation: *Can we afford to entertain all these nice folks?*

The positive side of agreeing on an estimated head count is that once you know the size of the wedding, you can move on to selecting and booking a reception site. You will quickly see why the cost of the reception is the largest chunk of the wedding expenses, a major reason why all parties contributing to its cost need to be involved in the final decision.

Research the possibilities

Modern technology has brought us the internet. Sit down in front of the computer and do a search on wedding reception sites for the area in which you plan to hold the wedding. I searched on "banquet menus and weddings" and on "wedding receptions," and clicked on "Connecticut" for a plethora of sites. Consider this a starting point, as all possibilities may not be listed for a particular area. You'll find photos, menus, and basic information on the type and size of wedding the site is accustomed to handling, and even info about date availability.

In addition to doing a web search for locations, check out the yellow pages of the telephone book. Look under "banquets" and under "restaurants." Don't limit yourself to your local phone directory. While on the road, stop by hotels or restaurants in towns that interest you but are out of your calling area, and turn to their yellow pages. Copy down names, addresses, and telephone numbers (it's not nice to rip out the pages) of places you want to check into.

Don't neglect the possibility of renting local visitor attractions, such as parks, old homes, museums, and historic sites. Although there will be more work involved in locating a caterer and providing such things as seating, linens, and dinnerware, your wedding will have the exact atmosphere your couple is looking for. Some lovely old mansions with stretching lawns make captivating spots for weddings. Were you aware that the famous Newport Mansions can be rented out for weddings? Rosewood, I know, offers an all-inclusive package from the band to the wedding cake. Just think! Your wedding pair can be photographed on the same spiral staircase used by Jamie Lee and Arnold in the movie *True Lies*.

Almost every golf club or hotel has banquet facilities, as do private clubs and unique sites, like wineries. We went to a wedding held at the ballroom at Foxwoods Casino in Ledyard, Connecticut that was lovely. Each guest received a chip as a favor and could duck out and gamble in between dances.

Peruse area bridal information guides and talk to people who have attended or given weddings. Ask and ask and ask. You may miss some fantastic places to have a wedding unless someone happens to mention them to you. For example, I know of a charming, privately-owned village in the backwoods of Connecticut called Johnsonville. The site's chapel and beautifully landscaped grounds used to be available on a limited basis for wedding rental. A unique location, like Johnsonville, may not be listed in the phone book; you might hear of it by word-of-mouth. If this type of place appeals to your couple, check with the Chamber of Commerce of the town in which you'd like to hold the reception.

Get on the horn

Prescreen potential reception sites with a phone call (rather than e-mail) to the banquet manager or person in charge of events. (Your son or daughter might handle such fact-finding calls, and you all can review the results.)

55

Anyone is liable to answer the phone, so ask the name of the person and his or her title to assure you aren't querying the kitchen helper. As we discussed, you'll be asked for an approximate guest count to determine if there is space to accommodate you. This call allows you to eliminate places that will be too small or too large. (If you have begun by checking the facility's web page, you might also learn this information.) For locations you are seriously considering, a live conversation will be more productive.

All of our weddings were that awkward size, 100 to 125 people. You'll find large banquet facilities consider anything under 150 people a "small" wedding. And, if you don't meet their minimum count, they may charge you a premium to host your wedding at their site. Many popular halls offer secondary rooms for smaller groups. Be sure you ask about this, should you visit the site. These second choices can be restrictive. Should a larger wedding be using the primary ballroom, terrace, and grounds, your group will not be allowed to share these areas with them.

Talk to others who have had events at a particular facility to find out if they were satisfied with the room they were provided and the management of their affair. I've heard stories of facilities with several event rooms pulling the old switcheroo. While you may have booked the grand ballroom, you may arrive to find your bridal tables set up in a lesser room because a more important event took precedence.

Another important question: how much time do they allow for set up between events? You won't want the leavings from a former party staying on for yours.

In the case of a site that requires you to bring in your own caterer, ask for the names of reputable companies who have served meals at that facility. These people are already acquainted with the personnel and know the general rules and procedures in putting out a meal there. If your choice site has a kitchen, great! But if your reception is in a park or held on a mountaintop, the caterer will need to arrive with his or her own kitchen on wheels.

When you contact a site that provides either its own caterer or has a restaurant, don't be shy about asking for an approximate per-person price range over the phone. This varies from one area to another. It costs more to put on a wedding in an affluent area, so if you live in New York City, say, be ready to swallow hard when you hear their estimate, and then to either chop down your guest list, switch to serving hamburgers, or look in the suburbs. You'd be surprised how many people on your list you can eliminate when you know it will cost $300 to invite each of them.

With a general idea of cost, you'll be able to rule out unsuitable places before you take the time to visit them (and the bride and groom get their hearts set on a place you can't afford). If, after this telephone conversation, you are still interested, ask the individual to e-mail, snail mail, or fax you a packet of information. Then make an appointment to tour the facility and obtain the details.

Make the rounds

With your luck, the bride and groom will want a typical wedding, just like those of their friends. Your guest count will be upwards of fifty people and, if you are paying the tab or invited along, you and the happy couple will be spending consecutive Saturdays riding around the countryside meeting with banquet or event managers. You will find it interesting that your bride is focused on the details of the wedding, while the groom is more worried about securing a proper job and finding them living quarters. If at least one of your couple is looking to the future, that's a good sign.

Here you all are, riding in the car. You have an itinerary based on reviews of packets you have received and are trying to fit in four appointments. The first place, you love (partially because it's reasonably priced) and they hate. It's too dark. The banquet manager was snotty. Well, maybe these things are true so you make a mental note to classify it as a last resort.

It is interesting to watch the couple's reaction as you enter place after place. After the first few, you can tell immediately whether you should spend more time at a facility. If a place is "right," you'll know it because the bride and groom will roam around it exclaiming how perfect it is. They'll envision their friends dancing and enjoying it. If the bride and groom can't picture themselves being there, cut that appointment short and go on to the next choice, because you are wasting precious time.

Consider the environment

Interior space can be deceptive. For an at-home reception held inside the main living area of your home, consider traffic flow to, from, and around the reception area. A circular pattern, where guests can move easily among the various areas, will help eliminate jam-ups. At every party I've hosted at my home, people collected in the kitchen. Find a way to block off this area to allow caterers or any hired help (or you) to tend to their duties without having to move bodies to open a refrigerator or check on food in the oven.

Because a home is configured differently than, say, a banquet hall, available dining and walking areas will be irregularly shaped, as opposed to a backyard area or wide-open, unencumbered banquet hall. Rearrange or remove furniture to free as much space as possible in areas your guests will frequent. If you plan to use a finished basement (recreation room) or a clear area in your backyard (hopefully under a tent or canopy), people will collect in a main area. In this case, your main concern will be traffic flow to the bar, food, and toilet facilities. Should you plan to host an after-wedding party or brunch in your home, apply these same restrictions.

For an external reception held at a banquet facility, consider the room's size and shape. Good facility event managers should know the crowd capacity of each room offered for parties, but it wouldn't hurt to second guess their estimates. Tables for gifts and displays, space for a DJ or band, and stations for a photographer and/ or a videographer consume space, as does a dancing area. You won't want seated guests jammed against a gift table or Grandma blasted by the music. If you've a choice, select a room large enough to give your guests breathing room.

How much room is enough?[16]
Ceremony: 8 sq. ft. / guest
Cocktails only: 8 sq. ft. /guest
Dining only: 10 sq. ft. /guest
Dancing only: 20 sq. ft. /couple
Cocktails & dancing: 10 sq. ft. /guest
Cocktails, dancing & serving stations: 12-13 sq. ft. /guest
Reception with dinner & dancing: 15-20 sq. ft. /guest

Space needed per guest x number of guests = total area needed for event

---

With a reception facility, everything must fall neatly into place and, most importantly, it should be affordable. Will the guests be separated into several rooms? Is the layout such that your guests need to switch rooms to dine and dance? Will they serve a sit-down dinner or only buffets? How is the ambiance? Contemporary or traditional? Does the room you're considering have poor acoustics—when you're in it, every sound seems to echo? Once filled, the noise level may become unbearable. Also, if the walls are thin, you might be fighting noise from a party in the next room.

Once your initial impression is satisfactory, there will be a slew of unanswered questions. Most bridal planners include fill-in-the-blank questions to ask the banquet manager. Getting the hidden details will ensure a complete understanding about what services and functions are included in the price quoted.

Watch the "watchdog"

When you and your children go facility hunting, your main contact will be the facility watchdog, the banquet or events manager. These folks can make your event a blast or a bomb, so steer your children (who are probably more forgiving than wise old you) toward a smart choice. Use your instincts and pay attention to negative signals. If you are directly involved in the reception hall selection and are paying for all or most of the expense, use your power to nix those with problem banquet managers. If not, communicating with your couple as they relate happenings can tip you off to potential issues.

Unreliability at the onset can spell disaster at the finale. Boot these folks at the start and keep searching until you are happy with the person who will be masterminding your event. Do they return calls the same day or the same month? Do you arrive for an appointment and have to wait an hour, or find you had been scheduled on their day off? When you ask for information, do you get it? Will they research a question and get back to you before you forget you even asked it? Did that packet of prices they swore they would send you ever arrive? Maybe they'll forget the date and time of your wedding, double schedule you with another event, or get your food order mixed up in the kitchen?

Inflexibility accompanying a bad attitude is a STOP sign. Do they act as if they are doing you a major favor by allowing you to have a wedding at their hall? Are they snippy and flippant over the phone? Do they meet simple requests with "can't do's?"

If you like a particular banquet manager, you are probably responding to a feeling of comfort and security. It's the old gut feeling that tells us something is right. Go with it. If you are uncomfortable with someone in charge either talk to his or her boss about reassigning another person to manage your event or go elsewhere. Half of your wedding budget is a lot of money to toss around lightly.

With our brood, we wound up with three entirely different types of reception sites, each reflected the personalities of the bride and groom. One daughter wanted a large, all-inclusive room where she could have a party atmosphere, so we found a popular restaurant with a large ballroom. Our other daughter preferred a feeling of intimacy and selected and old inn, where guests could wander from room to room and visit. As most guests were from out of town and required overnight sleeping quarters, the inn proved a perfect solution. We commissioned the entire facility, with its beautifully attired one-of-a-kind rooms, for the night so we could stumble upstairs to bed at the reception's end. My son, an avid golfer, and his fiancée selected a country club. The view was spectacular and the rolling lawns were cooling on our stocking feet after rounds and rounds of dancing in dyed-to-match pumps.

Analyze the reception package

The process of studying proposals is the same for each wedding vendor you consider. The most intricate proposal is the wedding package, as it is the overall event that is supported by smaller participating vendors, such as the photographer or videographer, florist, or baker.

What makes the reception package so complicated is that it involves making many decisions at once. Some can be delayed until closer to the wedding, yet certain hard decisions must be made at once or you won't have a clue about the potential cost of your event. Once you have narrowed down the location choices, consider the types of food and drink to be served and how you will serve them. Will guests be seated or standing? Will a meal be offered buffet-style or served?

If your couple is including you in the planning, they will appreciate your help and opinion—although they may not necessarily agree with you. The task at hand is to put pencil and calculator to work to estimate the total cost of the type of reception envisioned. Do this in a quiet place, because it requires concentration.

I like to start by figuring out the total cost per person for each prospective location, including all the extra and hidden costs not apparent in the flat rate. That way, if it's outrageous, we can dump the choice and move on. Gather all the information: the wedding packets from the facilities under consideration,

and all the notes and responses to questions from meetings. It's he
set up a spreadsheet comparing the offerings for each possibility. Read each
packet carefully to determine what is included. For facilities that provide an
all-inclusive package, check to see if tax and gratuities have been factored
into the cost. Are there any extras you'll need to pay for, such as bartenders,
restroom attendants, and valet parking?

Consider the bar package. Open or cash bar? Is a cocktail reception
included in the overall cost? How many hours before extra charges kick in?
Are top-shelf liquors included, or offered at a premium? If you will serve wine
with dinner, are the brands offered to your taste? If not, what is the corkage
fee to provide your own wine? What will happen if you cancel?

Some packages include a wedding cake and, possibly, a floral centerpiece
for the head table. Take each area of the packet and scrutinize it for what is *not*
included. Read the fine print. Look at the cost of hors d'oeuvres. These are
usually priced by quantity. Shrimp will cost more than stuffed mushrooms.
Filet mignon or lobster will be more expensive than chicken or fish.

In addition to cost considerations, you will be dealing with tugs of
conscience. You will likely lean towards choosing the least costly of the
sites you are reviewing, whilst your daughter or son is rooting for the most
expensive. This is normal. Negotiate. Think of this as a bonding time to
bring the reality of expenses to the forefront. To keep within your wedding
budget, compromise by inviting fewer people, serving chicken instead of
tenderloin, or finding ways to cut costs in another area. If you are having
a formal wedding and that punch and cookie reception is starting to seem
mighty good, it might be time to revisit your preliminary guest list and hack
away a few more names. We'll be fine-tuning that list soon, anyway.

Know that, in the end, your choice of site will be guided by its affordability,
the degree of formality it offers, the guest count you all anguished over, and
the wishes of the bride and groom.

Dear Joy,

I'd heard weddings cost a bundle, but this is ridiculous!

CHAPTER 8

Small Decisions, Big Money

P ART OF MAKING A WEDDING work is figuring out the best way to achieve the things you *all* want without ending up in bankruptcy court. Getting the pieces to fit smoothly into your budget is a juggling act. Once the ceremony and reception hall are booked, it will be easier to fuss with the remaining items. If you know, for example, that the cake is included in the reception cost, you can skip hunting down a baker. If the hall will be holiday-decorated, florist's expenses will be cut back.

Interview and analyze quotes from photographers, florists, and music sources just as you have the reception. While these costs will be less complex, they still bear scrutiny to avoid hidden fees and prevent problems. One of the most helpful books we used was *Bridal Bargains* by Denise and Alan Fields[17]. This tell-all book exposes pitfalls, alerts brides to moneymaking vendor schemes, and offers soup-to-nuts advice on how and where to get the best deals for anything from wedding favors to honeymoon spots. Buy this book and others like it on line or at a brick and mortar bookstore.

Where's Waldo?

Waldo is a fictitious cartoon character cleverly hidden in drawings. We played the "Where's Waldo" game of finding what was missing at weddings we attended. Did they give out favors? Have centerpieces ⌐ wine with dinner? It's amazing what folks *don't* notice.

At one wedding we attended, there was a major screw-up. ⌐ hadn't delivered the cake. Few of us, especially the ones who wer⌐ to the excellent band and enjoying the fruits of the open bar, were aware dessert hadn't been served. The people who will notice these things are crotchety Aunt Emily and the snobby neighbor down the street you felt obligated to invite. Your *real* friends will be having too good a time to care.

Cut the fluff that won't matter and focus on providing the things that are important to create the ambiance and mood you and your guests will enjoy and a day you'll all fondly remember.

Do-it-yourself

It may save you money to craft favors, bake your own wedding cake, make floral or table arrangements, or create and print out the wedding invitations; but will you have the time to do it without major stress? Time flies in the last months before the wedding. Commit only to a project you can manage, or your resentment will bode negative energy for the event.

"Friendly" photos

Uncle Harry may be the family photographer, but is his work good enough to put in an album to remember? Avoid trying to save money by using friends or relatives who dabble in photography to shoot the *primary* photos of your wedding. More often than not the pictures will not be as professional as you'd hoped, and there is no way to retake them without repeating the wedding. You may also kiss the relationship goodbye, should you express displeasure at the results. Taking photos is a job requiring that the photographer be everywhere and anywhere something is going on involving the bride and groom. Invite friends and family to take pictures as a *supplement* to your professional photographer and you'll eliminate potential grief.

The day will fly by so quickly that you'll hardly remember it, which is why it's important to spend the bucks on a reputable photographer to record memories for you. The best photographers book up fast, especially during popular wedding seasons, so make this decision as early as possible. The reliable referrals are from friends who have been happy with wedding photographs from a particular company. The results may be fine, but also ask how the person they used behaved. The photographer for my son's wedding was bossy and interfering. Were there conflicts between the photographer and the videographer, or resentment towards guests taking their own photos?

Whoever is paying for the photographer should interview at least three photographers in the company of the to-be-wedded couple. This decision is not only financial, but emotional. When (the collective) you visit the studio, peruse several albums to be certain the photographer is taking the types of photos the couple wants.

Each photographer will have a specific style. Eons ago, when I was married, we choose a photographer known for taking good candid shots. While you are in the shop flipping through sample albums, note whether the photographer takes set poses for all couples or if he or she appears to be sensitive to the wedding participants and truly captures the personality of the wedding. Be sure to ask for references from any photographer you are serious about hiring.

Price packages will vary to include a no-frills option—proofs and negatives only—to leather-bound, personalized albums. The more complete packages include a set of finished photos for the parents, as well. I have a collection of professional photos bound into a small parents' album, but the display style I enjoy most is a foldout composite frame that will stand up.

Most contracts are unbreakable without valid cause, so read the fine print before committing. If you hire a particular person, make sure the contract provides for an equally experienced alternative, should something prevent that individual from making the date. The owner of the company who was to photograph our son's wedding died beforehand. A minion was sent in his place. As this was a reputable company, the photos turned out fine. Should you have such a situation, you may not be as fortunate.

On tape?

While photos are beautiful, they are flat and still. There's nothing like a good video to capture the action of the day. Have copies made to send to loved ones who missed the wedding, so they can envision themselves being with you there.

Videotaping the wedding is optional; but, because it's a secondary means of recording the day's events, there is more flexibility. Hire a professional whose work you've seen and love, or accept the gracious offer of a friend or relative who wants to offer a wedding video as a gift.

Professional videographers will usually provide a demo tape of a wedding they've done. Avoid those who videotape trite scenes, such as those of the photographer taking photos of the wedding party. A videotape should capture the sacredness and liveliness of the event—the ceremony, the party, and the people having fun. Again, before you hire, ask for references, lest you end up with an inept bozo.

The videos we have enjoyed most were those taken by friends of the family. These folks were familiar with us and didn't merely focus on the wedding party. Not only did they film the ceremony, but we have a great collection of things we all said and did that bring us back to that day. My daughter plays their wedding video repeatedly, and my grandchild has come to enjoy it as if it were a movie. Each time they watch the event they uncover nuances, such as Dad doing the polka with Grandma, and Uncle Charlie pinching Aunt Emma's butt.

Table cameras

Disposable cameras are so inexpensive that it's worth it to set some around the reception site for guests to use. Discount stores frequently have sales. Some stores will discount a volume purchase. Our cameras resulted in some wonderful, hard copy, candid shots of friends and relatives that normally would not be included in a professional album. Be sure someone is in charge of collecting the cameras after the wedding, though, or you won't have these photos.

Plan to set a camera at each table, as well as in strategic places around the reception hall, so that folks can pick one up and snap a photo when they feel like it. You'll get all kind of quirky pictures to laugh over and enjoy, and you'll have them much sooner than the professional photos—which seem to take eons to obtain. I arranged our photos in a small album, which I carried around and inflicted on friends and acquaintances for weeks after the wedding.

Bear in mind that guests will also take photos using their cell phones or personal cameras. These will leave the reception with them. Do ask them to e-mail you copies to add to your collection.

Let there be music!

Music is needed for background, to create a mood, whether it is the organ played at the church or the thumping beat of rock music at the reception. Each couple will have specific preferences about the selections played or sung. My daughter listened to CDs for months before the wedding to find a repertoire of songs she and her fiancé wanted to express their day. It's up to your couple to prioritize the importance of each element. Hiring live people to sing and play costs money, so determine where this would be best suited. Some sort of music should accompany the ceremony, but do they really need violinists for the receiving line?

Often the church or synagogue has an in-house organist and can recommend a soloist. Check for limitations and special needs. Should your couple crave rap music or a washboard band for the ceremony, it would be wise for them to first discuss it with whoever is in charge of the venue. What are the acoustics? High ceilings distort sound, and there is little control over a screeching sound system. If your couple knows that a pricey music choice for the ceremony will not come across as beautifully as they'd like, they may opt for something simpler and spend the extra cash on a band or disc jockey (DJ) for the reception.

Most relatives or friends blessed with musical talent will be honored to be asked to sing or play at your wedding. Reward them by including them in prewedding events, such as the rehearsal dinner, and by providing them a corsage. Do offer to pay their standard fee, even though the person is apt to refuse it.

At a formal wedding where there will be dancing, music is essential. This is another decision that needs to be made early on. Good bands and DJs book up far in advance. Look for musicians who specialize in weddings, as they will be attuned to the flow of events. By the way, a DJ is no longer considered a low-cost option, because along with the music comes the same banter and patter typical of a bandleader. Their job is entertainment: to get people out on the floor dancing and to act as a master of ceremonies, providing the expected music and announcing key events—the first dance, cutting the cake, or tossing the bouquet.

As part of deciding on a particular band or DJ, the couple should make it a point to attend an event where this group or person is playing. Note how they play to the crowd and pace the music. A good entertainer will involve the audience and won't wait until the dance floor is crowded and in a rock-and-roll

frenzy to take a break or switch to mood music and bare the flo
a DJ, whom we had seen perform at a friend's daughter's wedding, a
not disappointed. This fellow had my husband wearing an Indian head
and leading a conga line around the hall to the tune of "Hot, Hot, Hot," and
we were all up dancing (even the oldsters) to "YMCA."

Eat cake

Traditional or not, it wouldn't be a celebration without a cake. A wedding cake not only adds to the festiveness of the occasion, but it doubles as a dessert after a meal, or as an accompaniment to coffee or tea at any sort of reception. Here's where we can be creative and cut corners. If the cake will be provided along with the wedding package at your chosen reception hall, you're home free.

For a small wedding, a suitable cake can be home-baked by you or a friend who enjoys cake decorating. Hunt through cookbooks or bridal magazines for recipes and tips, and find tiered cake pans and decorating supplies at party shops. If you will be making your own cake, give serious thought to storage and transport. Avoid using cream-based fillings and icings that require refrigeration. Delicate frostings, like whipped cream and meringue, won't hold up over time. Remember that the cake will need to be durable enough to sit out on display throughout the reception. Talk to bakers or do research to learn how to pack the cake for travel to avoid arriving with toppled tiers.

According to my favorite resource, *Bridal Bargains*[18], there are many ways to save money on cakes without doing your own baking, such as ordering cakes and decorations by mail, as well as tips on cheating on cake size without being caught.

Most of us go the easy route and order from a baker. In addition to pastry shops, there are also some excellent independent out-of-home bakers who specialize in cakes. Ask for local recommendations. Contact the baker or stop in at their shop to obtain a price quote—and a supply of cake samples. To this day, I remember stuffing our faces with delights bought home for tasting, such as chocolate raspberry layer cake.

Unless your bride is anti-tradition, she will plan to take home the top tier of their wedding cake and save it for their first anniversary to ensure she will have a loving and faithful husband (as the custom predicts). To prevent sawing through a stale cake one year later, the cake needs to be kept frozen. To prevent freezer burn, I recommend removing the cake, once it has frozen solid, from its cute little box and wrapping it tightly in aluminum foil. Return it to the freezer. Hopefully, there will be enough celebratory champagne at your daughter's or son's anniversary cake-cutting to make the cake taste just as delicious as they remembered it.

Flowering

Like the cake, flowers are integral to a wedding as they enhance the beauty of the ceremony and help carry out the theme and style of the event. Unless you are vying for a coveted florist on a popular date, it's okay to wait until three to six months before beginning florist selection. Usually, this is once the bride has selected her gown and decided on the bridesmaids' dresses. If available, bring photos or magazine tear-outs of the gown and color swatches to the meeting. Flowers may be fresh or artificial. The bride's decision will hinge on the type of the wedding, as well as the cost and availability of the quantity and variety she chooses.

For a small deposit, a florist will reserve a date. (The balance will be due a couple of weeks before the wedding.) Interview several and, as you narrow down the choice, check references. Ask if the florist had everything ready and delivered to the place indicated on time and if the flowers were fresh and as ordered.

Most folks opt to have flowers arranged by a professional florist. If you are a do-it-yourselfer with an artistic streak, think twice about taking on flower duty, especially if you will be using real flowers. Making up fresh bouquets for the event can be tricky, as the process requires some knowledge of when a flower bud will bloom and how long it will stay fresh. It wouldn't do to have brown-edged, wilted roses for the walk down the aisle.

A professional florist comes with the expertise of flowers and knows the availability and tolerance levels of each variety. When my daughter and I stopped in to visit one florist, we caught her in the act of readying lilies for a wedding. She had pails of them sitting in a bathroom to coax the buds open; the room was ablaze with lights and the shower ran steaming water. I can't say I'd have that much patience just before a wedding.

If you are using fresh flowers and one of the bridesmaids is allergic to pollen, speak to the florist about varieties that are pollen-free, low-pollen, or have removal pollen. Some choices might be budding roses, lilies, orchids, camellias, and hydrangeas.

The bride often has a general idea of the kind of flowers she wants to have for herself and her attendants, as well as the color of the bouquets. My Linda was set on fresh tulips, yellow ones. The problem we had was that tulip season ended just before her wedding, so the color choice was limited and the cost of tulips was higher than it would've been a week or two earlier. No matter how specific your bride may be about the exact kind and color of flower to go into the bouquets, with real flowers florists are restricted by what their suppliers have available at the time the order is filled.

Our florist had the courtesy to call to let Linda know white and cream tulips would need to be mixed into the "yellow" bouquets. Her sister and I lit lavender candles and made Linda sip chamomile tea to calm her down. Brides are so emotional just before a wedding. When the bouquets were delivered to our home the morning of the wedding, they were perfect—except for the pink flowers that had worked their way into the arrangement. "I told them, no pink!" (More tears, more tea.)

Go silk!

While there's nothing like the fragile beauty and natural scent of fresh flowers, there is much to be said for using artificial ones. Many florists who handle fresh arrangements also deal with silk. High-quality silk flowers are a close stand-in for the real thing. They can even be scented to duplicate the smell of, say, a rose. The bride can choose her favorite flower/s in whatever color/s she wishes without concern for seasonal availability or worry about them wilting in the steamy heat of summer or shriveling in winter's cold.

Not only are silk bouquets more lightweight than fresh ones, but they are easier to handle and transport. They can survive being dropped, stepped on, or squashed into a box and do not require water to stay fresh. And, they are pollen free, so your bridesmaid won't be sneezing at the altar.

Keep in mind that while silk wedding flowers can be more practical than real flowers, they can also be just as expensive, if not more so. While you may pay less for exotic or out-of-season flowers, a silk version of a more common flower is apt to cost more than its real counterpart.

Decorate with Flowers

It's easy to become so carried away with flowers that your event smells like a funeral parlor. Put arrangements at eye level, where they will be noticed, such as at the entrance to the reception. Use the *Where's Waldo* approach to figure out places flowers won't be missed. Do you need them at each table? Will anyone care if there are none in the restroom?

There are many devious ways to save money on flowers. One gal successfully decorated with supermarket flowers. Use bridal party bouquets to decorate tables where the wedding party is seated, in lieu of a centerpiece. Flowers for the church can be transported for use at the reception hall. If you do this, arrange for the florist to make the switch.

Many times, a reception facility has a list of florists they work with, and some halls may even include an arrangement for the head table in their package. Use the same strategies for decision-making: look for reliability, commitment, and firm quotes that won't leave you at the altar minus the boutonnières.

Set the table

This brings us to the necessity of centerpieces. It's easy to anguish over what to put at the center of each table. You might settle on flowers, lanterns, candles, or something simpler. A large centerpiece can become a problem once food arrives at a table and guests can't see each other over it. Something small and elegant will be much more appropriate, and won't crowd the food off the table.

Any facility or restaurant that hosts banquets uses some sort of table decoration. Find out what is available. At one wedding, we borrowed hurricane globes with a candle in the center. We asked our florist to set some green fern leaves under the lamp; it looked pretty and cost a pittance.

While white is traditional for a formal wedding, you may be offered a choice of tablecloth and napkin colors, which will allow you to extend the color theme of the wedding. If you are having the affair catered and need to bring in linens, you will have color choices, as well.

Do you really need a favor?

A custom in our Italian family was giving out white tulle packets containing Jordan almonds as wedding favors. The giving of five Jordan almonds represents the five wedding wishes for health, wealth, long life, fertility, and happiness. Their candy-coating symbolizes the bitter and the sweet of marriage.[20]

I relayed this tidbit to my first daughter, and talked her into doing the almond thing. We all sat at our dining room table one Sunday morning counting and wrapping the dang things to the tune of 200 bundles. It was boring; it was tedious. A taste test confirmed the almonds were stale. That was the last time I interfered with the favor selection. My next daughter settled on two heart-shaped chocolates that came prepackaged in a tiny gold box.

A favor for each guest is certainly a nice touch, especially if you can offer one that is meaningful enough for guests to treasure. At one wedding, we received a recorded CD of the couple's favorite songs. At another, a flower girl handed each female guest a single rose.

The heartbreak is that the favors that we spend so much time and money on, even the edible ones, are often forgotten on the table. So the question is *do we really need them at all?* The sad truth is that with all the food and drink served, favors often become buried in the leftovers. And, really, who needs personalized commemorative napkins, matches, and other trinkets that will ultimately end up as junk drawer clutter?

Steer your daughter toward practicality and help her save money by deciding if favors will truly enhance the wedding, or if they simply will be table ornaments.

Wheels

Of course you will need a decent vehicle or two to squire around the wedding party for the day. A clean, shiny car driven by a volunteer friend or relative will do nicely—and it's free for the price of a car wash and a tank of gas.

Your other option is to hire a limousine or party bus. Your daughter will have preferences. We talked Mary into a party bus because the ceremony was an hour from home and the bus was equipped with a restroom—a female necessity. Linda would settle for nothing less than a limo. We needed to rent two limos to accommodate the bride, her parents, and the bridesmaids.

Reliability is important if the bride is to get to the church on time. If you are using a friend as a driver, be sure he or she is the punctual sort. Most companies providing transportation set their reputation on punctuality. To be sure, check references and use referrals before contracting. You may need to book a limo a year in advance, depending on where you live. Allow time to review several companies and to check out their vehicles in person.

Some companies charge a portal-to-portal fee, which is the time it takes them to drive from their office to your home. Read the contract and make sure everything you agree upon is in writing. The contract should state the color and year of the vehicle and size and number of passengers it will carry. Make sure the car you see is the car you are going to get to avoid having an older model show up.

Getting to the church

In olden days, the way a bride got to church and to her new home afterward was cloaked in superstition. It was thought that if a bride walked to church there was more chance of her seeing good omens. A rainbow, sun shining on the bride, and meeting a black cat or a chimney sweep were all considered lucky. Bad omens included seeing a pig, hare, or lizard run across the road, or spotting an open grave. Seeing minks or nuns foretold barrenness and a life of dependence on charity.

Returning from church, a new wife must enter her home by the main door and must never trip or fall to avoid bad luck. Thus, the custom of carrying the bride over the threshold.[21]

Send out invitations

When and if you are asked for your input, be honest, but tactful. Wedding invitations, whether sent on line, printed, or engraved, are an expression of the bride and groom and a preamble to the wedding. Your daughter or son might have different tastes than you, but this doesn't mean their choice isn't right or that it won't be just as nice. Allow yourselves plenty of time. For e-invites, you'll need to acquire e-mail addresses; hard copy invitations need to be addressed and assembled.

No matter which delivery system you choose, be sure to send out the invitations at least two months in advance of the wedding. A wedding invitation is normally formal and, as such, needs to be the epitome of correctness. If your circumstances are such that the wording of the invitation is not the straightforward, "Mr. & Mrs. Jones cordially invite you to the wedding of their daughter . . .," consult the newest edition of *Emily Post's Wedding Etiquette*[22] for the correct wording for your particular situation. In the invitation packet, be sure to indicate a rain date for outdoor weddings *sans* canopies and to include travel directions and maps for guests.

E-invitations

Don't freak out if your couple decides to send invitations via e-mail. E-invites are the most economical and eco-friendly way to make short work of the task. In addition to saving time, energy, paper, and postage these systems are set up to handle on-line responses. Many times, an invite system is part of a website the couple sets up to handle other facets of the event, such as gift registries. If you haven't checked out the on-line invite option yourself, I recommend you take a quick gander at companies like Paperless Post and Cocodot.[23] The couple can design and personalize an invitation that will be a close match to the traditional one they might send via snail mail and save money. Should the to-be-weds take this route, they will need to print out and mail invitations to relatives and friends who might not have stepped up to the digital age.

Traditional paper invitations

Handwritten invitations are fine for a very small wedding, but as the guest list grows, this can bring on writer's cramp. Most invitations are printed today, rather than engraved, as new printing techniques have made it impossible to tell the difference. Computers and pre-printed notepaper have made doing-it-yourself easy. If your son or daughter is clever and has the time and patience, it's possible to create and print out distinctive, professional-looking invitations using on line programs for a fraction of the printed cost.

Do you need to pay extra to have the outer envelope addressed by a calligraphist? While this is a nice touch, it is costly. There is nothing wrong with a neatly hand-addressed envelope. If your son or daughter is computer savvy, it's easy enough to print out the envelopes. My daughter was able to duplicate the font used on the invitation. Also, there are many script fonts to choose from that look lovely.

Another consideration is the cost of postage. It's customary to enclose a stamped, self-addressed envelope for the response. But understand that the weight of the entire package might entail using two or more stamps on the outer envelope. Consider this when you opt for heavyweight stationary or double-lined envelopes.

Before stamping the invitations, make certain you are using the correct postage, lest the entire batch be returned and need to be restamped. Take an assembled invitation to the post office to determine the necessary postage or weigh it on a postal meter at the office.

Save-the-date cards

If the wedding is during the holidays or vacation season, it is smart to send out "save the date" cards to those you feel will need to make travel plans or other arrangements. Send these out at least six to eight months before the wedding, especially for a destination wedding.

If your couple has money in the budget, they might want to consider having save-the-date photo magnets printed up. And, of course, there is the good old-fashioned United States Postal Service. Using a postcard will save postage, as postcards cost about one-third less to mail than sealed envelopes. Create postcards on computer or handwrite them. I recently received a decorative save-the-date note via e-mail attachment, which I had to print out and worry about losing. Be aware that your notice could become buried in the invitee's e-mail bucket or, worse, relegated to spam.

Other printed matter

There are always extras to consider. One elaborate wedding we attended had elegant menus accompanying each dinner plate. We had some very nice wedding programs made up that listed the order of events and the names and function of anyone participating in the ceremony. Ushers usually hand them out as folks enter the ceremony facility for the wedding.

Should you want something other than the standard issue provided by ceremony or reception sites, create your own one-sheet flyers or foldout programs on a home computer, Print them out or have them photocopied. Bear in mind that quality paper costs more than 20-pound copy paper.

Wedding announcements

An announcement is sent after the wedding as a simple statement that a marriage has occurred. Some folks who have not been issued an invitation may be interested in hearing about your son's or daughter's nuptials. Suppose your daughter spent some time in Hong Kong. She might have friends there with whom she wants to share the news. Use discretion about sending an announcement to anyone who might have been expecting an invitation to the wedding and didn't receive one.

Thank-you notes

Gifts will begin arriving for the prospective bride and groom from the time the engagement is announced. Yes, I know, you are not responsible for writing thank-you notes for gifts the bride and groom receive. However, you are subject to the repercussions from friends and relatives if thank-yous are not received in a timely manner. Most people will feel awkward about phoning the bride to find out if she received their gift; they may call you instead.

I must be old-fashioned in that I feel sending a thank-you via e-mail (or worse, text message) is a cop-out. Certainly, it's done and is better than not receiving *any* acknowledgement of the receipt of a gift. If possible, thank-you notes should be mailed within a month of the receipt of a gift to provide instant acknowledgment to the giver and prevent hurt feelings. It's rumored that the bride has up to a year after the wedding to mail out thank-you notes. I feel that waiting such a long time to respond is an insult to the giver, who was nice enough to shop for a gift or to buy a nice card and write out a check to help the married couple start their lives. I still wonder if my friend's daughter ever received the crystal bowl I had sent from Tiffany's, and the girl has been married several years now.

With a daughter, it's easy enough to apply the guilt trip, "Have you sent a thank-you to Cousin Itt yet?" In the case of a daughter-in-law, you'll need to take the circuitous route through your son. For gifts received *en masse*, as in a bridal shower, suggest to the bride that she mail out thank-yous in one batch. After one of our larger showers, a cousin was irate when other relatives received a thank-you note long before she did. The bride and groom are busy; they have jobs and are trying to get their lives in order. Taking care of obligations is part of it.

Dear Joy,

My teenager is acting like a spoiled child and my husband has become a tyrant. Should I move out?

CHAPTER 9

It's All in the Family

WHILE YOU AND YOUR HUSBAND have been agonizing over all the cost issues, something special has been happening: you and your child are in close communication. You may already have such a relationship and the wedding plans have only served to enhance it, or this might be a new experience.

As parents, we have become accustomed to not having our kids around much. They have graduated from school and moved into their own apartments. They call, write, and visit, but they are no longer underfoot. Our conversations become laconic; we talk about less personal things, like the weather, and we don't *dare* ask with whom they are sleeping. So here we are with a wedding to plan and they are in our faces. Our tranquil life is spiked with frantic phone calls and babbling about dresses and sticky situations. We love it. We are needed again!

When our first daughter became engaged, it triggered a chain of visits and calls. She lived out-of-state, so we discussed vital issues and planned weekend excursions to bridal shops, photographers, and reception halls. My "dance card" was full for the first few months after her engagement as we worked on finalizing decisions on these major items. How I treasured that time, even though much of it was filled with the angst of a daughter who wanted the moon on a shoestring budget. But we've already covered sticker shock. The important thing is I had my daughter back. We worked through each obstacle as it occurred; I never could have predicted many of them. We'd get hung up for weeks trying to figure out how to deal with family situations. Just fine-tuning the wedding list required a million e-mails and phone calls.

Keeping Dad calm

Throughout this entire hubbub dear old Dad is making sobbing noises. He feels this whole wedding thing is out of control—his control. At this point, it's crucial to treat him gently. After all, the father of the bride or groom is an important part of this whole deal.

If you are marrying off a son, this is a wonderful bonding time for him and his dad. Dad will also be happier to shell out money when called for, because he knows he is getting off easy (especially if the bride's parents will take the biggest hit). Dad will feel he can be selective about what he wishes to do, so his son's wedding isn't much of an obligation.

Now a daughter, that's different. Dad has always been so overprotective. Here is his sweet little flower and this "person" is going to take her out of his protective realm. A sensitivity goes on here that we women often overlook. We have a tendency to shunt Dad off to the side so we can get on with our business. Most of it, he'd rather we handle. Dad hates to shop and doesn't have the patience for fussing with small details. The solution is to make Dad feel a part of things, but don't avalanche him with minor details, like the cost of the wedding gown you've chosen. You will pay it in installments, anyway.

What he really wants to know is, "How much?"

What Dad is going to keep asking you is what you might not know yet, *how much is the entire event going to cost?* You can hedge on that subject for a while, but showdown time is bound to come. And it will be when you least expect it. Include him in the budget-making process if you feel he can be part of it without having a heart attack. Stay price-conscious from the beginning. If you are exceeding the budget, be aware of it. Understand that no matter what the cost, Dad will always think it's too much to spend. It's not that he's a cheapskate; it may be he is simply unaware of the costs of clothes, food, and extraneous things that are not part of his world.

Many married couples have spoken or unspoken agreements on how much one of them can spend without first consulting the other. In your family, this amount may be $100, $500, or $1,000. Keep this in mind when you are finalizing your wedding cost decisions. My arrangement with my husband regarding major purchases goes like this. If it is something like a new car, my husband does most of the preliminary research and narrows down the selections for me and we both agree on the purchase.

Some cost commitments, like the reception hall, are as substantial as car purchases. Your husband may not wish to truck around with you to seek out a reception site, but he will want to approve it before you commit. Offer to take him to a place you all love for a final meeting. Drive by it and stop in with him. Have dinner there one night and sample the food. If Dad knows what he is paying for he will be much more comfortable with the decision.

One expenditure on which I insisted my husband be included was our daughters' wedding gowns. I waited until we had honed in on one or two, and then took him with us for the final buy. If my husband doesn't like the way something looks, he is often right. Involving Dad in this decision may not only keep you from making a serious mistake, but it will make him feel valued.

Buying a wedding gown is a very emotional process for a parent. There is not a one of us who hasn't shed a tear when we see our daughter in full wedding regalia. We know when it's the right dress, because we cry harder when we see her in it. Your husband needs to share this experience with you. A side benefit is he won't care what it costs. He'll pay it.

We forget about Dad in all the bustle of planning a wedding, and sometimes he wants us to. But he *does* care, and it's important to remember that, even though he may act nonchalant. Men show emotion in different ways than women do. Give them some attention and watch them bloom. Ignore them, and they will shrink and take it out on you by being gruff, like little boys looking for attention. A daughter and her dad are such a special combination. This may be, after all, the last time he will have his little girl all to himself.

Your other children

Sibling rivalry is as old as time. It stands to reason that when one person in the family is getting all the attention, the others will vie for it too. The bride's sister, your "other" daughter, will make a grand entrance at a prewedding party wearing low-slung jeans with thong underwear peeping out and a bandeau that barely covers her breasts. Your teenaged son, not the one being married, purposely stays out past his curfew with nary a call to you. Human nature deems these events and others like it will occur at the worst possible time—when Grandma is visiting or you've a houseful of company.

Recognize any behavioral changes for what they are: pleas for attention. You've dealt with this all your life and tried to make each of your children feel equally important and treated them so. Now that your time and emotions are so stressed, it's hard not to shirk duties to your other children so you can focus on helping the neediest, the one getting married. Are you leaving family members to fend for themselves for dinner while you go out with your to-be-wed daughter or son to interview photographers? Invite sisters and brothers of the bride or groom to be part of the planning, not useless appendages. Encourage them to help by assigning them small tasks. Ask their opinions. Make them feel as important as they truly are.

If a brother or sister will not be chosen as an usher or a bridesmaid, do what you can to quell any resentment. So much needs to be done on a wedding day that I'm sure you can find an important job to assign them. There are grandparents who need help getting around, children who need babysitting, boutonnières to distribute, and flyers that need handing out. Convince them that they are the best individuals for the job and they will be putty in your hands.

Should you or your husband have children from a previous marriage, be aware that they will be even more sensitive about being included in events than children born of both of you. Take care not to allow them to feel left out. Part of being a parent is splitting ourselves many ways to handle all of our children's needs. You can do it. I know you can!

Family obligations

All the quirks and quacks in the involved families surface. An arrogant sister or brother refuses to attend on religious grounds. Relatives who haven't spoken in years now must share the same room, maybe even the dinner table. No family is flawless. Weddings, like funerals, bring all the raw emotions and problems to a peak that sits there on your face like a pimple ready to be popped. And when it does, it can make an ugly mess before it heals and things are smooth again.

A mother-of-the-bride friend, who had severed communications with her family years prior, decided it was time to end the cold war and invited them all to the wedding. The bride had placed her long-lost grandpa, aunts, and uncles on the wedding list. All responded they would attend, so my friend arranged prime seating for them at her table and nearby. Only half of her family actually showed up.

My friend touched home that one day and was disappointed. We all have stones we dare not leave unturned, yet by taking an emotional risk who knows? Sometimes there's a happy ending. In this case, my friend's olive branch to her estranged family might've restored them to her.

These situations—every family has its unique ones to tolerate—can make or break this special day. After my mom and dad passed away, I lost contact with the uncles, aunts, and cousins who had been part of my life growing up. Theoretically, I didn't need to invite them to our daughter's wedding because our lives had become separate.

As in all families, there are always some folks you love and some you can't stand: the cranky aunt who delights in stirring up a nest of trouble with her razor-sharp comments; the cousin who drinks himself to into oblivion then falls asleep face-down in his dinner plate; and the aunt who shows up dressed like a hooker. We all have been embarrassed by folks like this. Because I was distanced enough to pick and choose without retribution, I guiltlessly crossed these offensive people off our list. As a result, I enjoyed a wonderful reunion that reestablished my relationship with relatives I cared for.

Your situation may not permit you the luxury of exclusion. You may feel obligated to invite undesirable relatives and family friends for your parents' sake. It's the old extended family syndrome. If you invite one cousin, you must invite them all or so-and-so will get offended and your parents will lose face. We spend so much time worrying over other people's feelings that sometimes we forget whose are really important—the bride's and groom's. Why do we allow ourselves to be manipulated by people who are not paying the bill?

If your extended family is close enough that you celebrate holidays together and call and visit often, you will probably want to include them all (down to your least favorite people) to maintain family harmony. Everyone will expect to be invited, so if you need to make cuts you will likely do it by levels: all aunts and uncles, no cousins; cousins, but no second cousins; no children under sixteen. A discreet phone call to a favorite uncle or aunt about your decision to cut a relative may ease the blow. Blame it on lack of funds.

"We'd love to have everyone, but it is soooo expensive." If the wedding is intimate, "only immediate family" may work as an excuse. Another is that you have "no control over the list," which they won't believe.

If you are the mother of the groom and your family is large, this is a good time to offer to pay for extra meals. You may be thanked and then turned down by gracious hosts, but that's okay. You've covered your base. Your new son or daughter-in-law probably has endured visits with the oddballs in your family by now so they know the score. They won't expect perfection, so invite these people and don't worry about it. Your integrity is intact.

How about exes?

And worst of all, especially if you have remarried, what about the birth father or the birth mother? Where do they fit in? There may have been no contact with these individuals in years, but you can be sure when there is confetti in the air that their names will come up. Here is this person, back in your life. A presence you may have to deal with on a special day. The net of it is that they are the natural father or mother of the bride or groom. That you disapprove of them won't matter. Your child may still want them to attend or to participate in the wedding.

My husband is my children's stepfather. A sticky situation arose when my daughter insisted that her birth father, who had dropped out of her life until she graduated college, be part of the after-ceremony receiving line. I could envision my husband, who had literally raised my children, standing nearby and listening to this man greet people with, "Hi. I'm Mary's dad." In a matter of minutes, there would be a knock-down-drag-out fight between the two men. I just knew it. After several weeks of an impasse on the subject between my daughter and me, we settled on having her birth dad do a reading at the service instead.

There are a couple of scenarios you may run into if you are dealing with an ex-somebody.

Scenario One: This person has remained a good parent, even though you have been divorced. He or she has spent time with the child and contributed to his or her upbringing. Your child loves this person. Sorry, you're stuck. This individual will be right alongside you in the receiving line sharing your glory. A father will give the bride away and a mother will be sitting up front with you participating in the ceremony. You will need to endure their presence at all preparatory events—showers, stag parties, and rehearsal dinners. Hey, wouldn't it be nice if they offered to pay for the wedding?

Scenario Two: This person has a problem. He or she may be lush, a two-timer, and/or a perpetually unemployed loser. Your biggest beef is that he or she has spent little or no time with your child—until now. Birthday and holiday gifts have been non-existent and this individual has contributed nothing to your child's life but disappointment. Your child knows this person exists and feels an obligation. Expect that this person will be on the invitation list. If you are lucky, your son or daughter won't feel guilty enough to ask him or her to participate in the ceremony.

His chickie-poo

Wait, it can get worse. Best case, your ex has remarried and you like his new wife better than you like him. Understand that both will attend the wedding as a couple. The problem occurs when he either has married or is living with the woman who broke up your marriage. You are so vicious about this relationship that you can't fathom having it in your face throughout this happy time of your life. You want to call this woman and tell her not to come, that she would be unwelcome. Yet, etiquette says you must swallow the bad stuff and say nothing if your ex chooses to bring her as his guest.

Don't let this spoil your day. Be a big enough person to tolerate the lunk and his appendage, but hold your ground on the important things. The kids have enough stress without adults acting like two-year-olds. The friction between you and your ex creates a problem for your child, so do your darndest to be flexible. You only need to be mildly cordial, and there will be so much going on that you can practically ignore the two of them. As payback, seat them with your most obnoxious relatives.

Dear Joy,

I thought this would be fun, but I find myself being resentful.

CHAPTER 10

People Picking

WHEN A BRIDE AND GROOM take the long white road down the aisle, they want to surround themselves with the special people in their lives—brothers and sisters, best friends, mentors, a favorite aunt or uncle, grandparents, and of course their parents. First, they must identify who these people are, and then they will map out where and how these folks fit into the wedding agenda.

The wedding party

Once your couple has basic plans in place, it's time to choose attendants and other ceremony participants. Suggest to your couple that they extend invitations as early as possible, especially if this will be a destination wedding, to allow people time to arrange schedules. By inviting early, there will also be time to find replacements for those who, for various reasons, are unable to do the honors.

Who will "give her away"?

Let's start with the bride, as this partner is the most emotionally complex. Today's young lady will probably bristle at the thought of being "given away," as if she were a possession, but I'm sure she would prefer to be walked down the aisle by a cherished person. It's a matter of semantics, but she is symbolically and physically being handed over to the groom. And it is considered an honor to be asked by the bride to be the one to do so.

We touched earlier about the role of Dad. In the typical family, there is only one person that answers to that qualifier. In many families there may be two or none. In a traditional wedding, a daughter asks her father or a father figure in her life to do the deed. Today, this isn't as simple. It doesn't have to be a man. She could choose both parents, just her mom, or even a favorite relative or friend. An older bride may want to walk herself down, as she feels beyond the stage where anyone should be "giving her away." Should the bride decide on a non-traditional alternative, try to be accepting and open-minded about it.

The best man or woman for the job

Who is going to stand up for them? While this is not your decision and it's normally none of your business, you may be the listening post. If you are so privileged, use common sense and diplomacy to guide your child through this delicate process. Sometimes the decision about whom to include in the wedding party is straightforward. Often, it's not.

Wedding Party Origins

The tradition of having a "best" man dates back to 200 A.D., when the bride was abducted from her home. The prospective groom took along his "best" man, a warrior friend, to fight off other men who wanted the woman and to prevent the woman's family from resisting. By Anglo-Saxon times, the two-man show grew to posse proportions and the groom called on many friends, called bridesmen or brideknights. It became the duty of the bridesmen to see that the bride got to the ceremony on time, and then to the groom's home afterward.

Bridesmaids or brideswomen appeared to assist the bride, once weddings became more of a planned event than a kidnapping. We have surpassed these barbaric beginnings, but held to choosing a best man and a maid or matron of honor to stand up with the bride and groom, as well as a wedding party of bridesmaids and ushers to further assist at and adorn the event.[24]

Attendants

By breaking the constraints of tradition, brides and grooms of today are truly able to have whomever they wish as attendants. The number of attendants on the bride's side no longer needs to match the same number as the groom's. The "maids" could very well be matrons or men. The best "man" might be a woman. And a wedding may have more than one maid of honor or more than one best man. The only rule, other than any religious constraints deemed by a particular church or synagogue, is that these people are the personal choices of the bride and groom. Don't you wish things were so flexible when you got married?

Your daughter or son will worry over who to ask and how to set up the procession. My son had, and still has, many friends. He solved his dilemma by selecting eleven as groomsmen, or ushers, and then found duties for several more. (All those handsome men. My, they looked good in those tuxes.) His bride had six attendants. They paired off a couple of sets of men at the end to even up the procession for the ceremony. My daughter settled on having two maids of honor, rather than chose between her two best buddies. We went to a smaller wedding, eighty people, with only a best man and a maid of honor. It was simple and lovely, and the attire didn't need to be bought or rented in bulk.

Set your old-fashioned thinking aside and work with your child on any attendant issues. Your son or daughter will be concerned about hurting someone's feelings by not including him or her. He or she may feel obligated to invite brothers, sisters, cousins, and members of the prospective in-laws' immediate family to join the wedding party and bypass asking a long-time friend. Help your son or daughter feel comfortable with his or her decision. Don't propagate feelings of guilt, and soften up on the "shoulds."

No doubt, issues will arise that will affect a bridesmaid's or usher's ability to participate. Being in a wedding party is expensive. When you invite someone to be an attendant, the duty means more than having them as a central figure in the wedding event. They will need to dedicate time and a good deal of money, even for a scaled-down event. Bridal party gear is expensive, whether it's bought or rented. Travel to and from events is costly and time consuming. And then there are the gifts for all the prewedding events—showers, stags—culminating in a substantial wedding present for the happy couple. The person may be willing, but their bank account may not be able to support this. Reiterate these obvious excuses to your child in hopes he or she won't feel put out if an invitation to participate has been turned down.

Married bridesmaids (I guess they officially would be bridesmatrons) may become pregnant, creating havoc with the dress situation; and if the baby's due date is around wedding time, the person may opt to back out of the duty entirely—which happened to one of my daughters.

Sometimes, it's an issue of appearance. A bride can get selfish and toy with not asking a good friend, so as to maintain a "pretty" wedding party. If she does this, you need to set her straight at once. Guide your children toward choosing attendants for what they mean to them, not by their looks or by obligation.

Caution your daughter or son to weigh seriously the consequences of asking friends or relatives who are known sots, on drugs, or experiencing psychiatric difficulties to join the wedding party. One bad apple could spoil the ceremony. You can't control the behavior of other people. You can only anticipate it and hope it doesn't interfere with the event. And lastly, be careful not to get in the middle of issues between the bride or groom and their wedding party attendants. They're old enough to settle these things themselves.

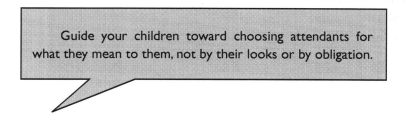

Guide your children toward choosing attendants for what they mean to them, not by their looks or by obligation.

Cute kids join the party

Wee flower girls and ring bearers are adorable, and can easily steal the show. Perhaps the bride or groom has a child, niece, or nephew they'd love to include in the wedding party. This child will feel very special, and I'm certain will be on best behavior. Be sure to extend a wedding invitation to the children's' parents, so these little ones can be monitored and will feel secure. My grandson was asked to be ring bearer in several weddings when he'd just turned five years old. I have a darling photo of him in his miniature tuxedo.

Fine-tune the guest list

Another kind of people picking pertains to wedding invitations. The guest list becomes an immediate item of conflict because each guest represents money and space. It pays to be selective. Once the dust has settled, you'll need to fine-tune your guest list to arrive at an actual head count, the expected number of attendees at the wedding. You will, no doubt, work around the capacity of the reception facility, as well as your budget constraints.

When you began reception hall hunting, there were issues; now there will be arguments. Unless you are paying for half the wedding, your plentiful roster of relatives and friends may be holding a sit-in on your front lawn because you couldn't invite them. You may decide to have a pre or postwedding reception of your own in hopes that these nice people will still speak to you.

We had such a situation at our son's wedding, minus the sit-in. I handed over what I thought was a reasonable list of attendees to my son, confident, after having just gone through our daughters' weddings, that it had been properly pared down. It was rejected. He had already put his own list together and some of our closest friends weren't on it. I alerted these folks to our lack of control well in advance of the wedding and tried to compensate by including them in another function. Still, one couple never understood why my son chose not to invite them. (I couldn't tell them that it was because of the time they insulted his fiancée.) These (former) friends have not exchanged a civil word with us since. Expect a few battle scars from being involved in a wedding, so be careful how you handle things.

A guest list has a life of its own, growing as plans progress. Doesn't it know it must stop once the deposit is made on the reception hall? It's wise to plan on last-minute attendees, and to understand that there will also be no-shows. We had a relative who insisted on bringing her grandchildren. Parents who can't find sitters are apt to show up with their kids, or a friend may assume she can bring a date.

The most horrifying situation I've heard about happened to a friend who gave her daughter an elaborate wedding at her home and served whole lobsters as entrees. Several people who had declined the invitation decided to show up to "surprise" the bride. Lobsters don't stretch that far, so the immediate family members gave up their dinners so as not to embarrass the party crashers. Someone in that group should've had the good sense to have alerted a bridesmaid—which wouldn't have spoiled the fun, but might've ensured enough food for all.

Establish rules and stick to them during the invitation response stage, or you risk offending someone who was nice enough to not to be pushy about bringing uninvited guests or children. It's hard to turn away uninvited guests, once they have arrived, dressed and ready for the party.

Work through the issues

Come to an agreement about whom and how many each invitation will include. The best way to avoid hard feelings is to make cuts by levels: no co-workers, no third cousins. If you don't know the name of the guest you expect an invitee to bring, perhaps this person isn't close enough to the invited guest to be included.

Should singles bring dates?

If you limit guests of single women and men to those who have serious relationships—engaged or longtime commitments, perhaps you can avoid having a maidenly aunt show up with her niece or current paramour. Be thoughtful about this decision, though. In an effort to limit the guest list for an elaborate wedding, the bride in a wedding I attended did not include the boyfriends, girlfriends, and fiancés of the wedding party. This created sore feelings amongst the attendants, as they were the focal point of the wedding. All gussied up and missing a loved one at a romantic couple's event.

You're invited, but . . .

It could easily be taken as an insult to be asked to attend *only* the ceremony, as it implies that a person is not important enough to be included in the entire event. Years ago, there were many hard feelings when wedding invitations were extended to people in tiers: close friends and relatives; regular friends and distant relatives; and acquaintances. The responses also required a great deal of management and organization. Card inserts denoted which other events, if any, that the invitee might attend. An invitation to the reception meant that guests were invited for the dancing and to share the wedding cake *after* the meal was served to the hard-core guests. It's understandable that, to my knowledge, this type of tiered wedding invitation is no longer issued. Today, what we call the reception is comprehensive, including food and entertainment. Either you are invited to the wedding or not.

Children?

Decide your policy toward children, and stick to it. As cute as children are, crying babies and chatty toddlers can ruin the mood of the wedding ceremony. When small children become restless, they pick fights with each other or may play hide and seek under the reception tables, leaving their meals mostly untouched. Don't be quick to make an exception. Some parents will be huffy if their children or other guests of their household are omitted from the invitation. So be it. Remember that these people are guests; guests don't dictate the rules or pay the bill.

I'm not saying you shouldn't invite children, but know the kind of children who might attend and plan accordingly. If children are included, make special arrangements with your caterer or the restaurant staff to provide kid-friendly foods, such as macaroni and cheese, burgers or dogs and fries, and to serve beverages in spill-proof, unbreakable containers. Set age limits. Provide parents enough time to secure an at-home sitter, or be nice and hire an on-premise sitter to keep the children entertained and in control while their parents enjoy the festivities.

Obligations

Just because you were invited to *their* daughter's wedding doesn't mean you must invite them to *your* event. The nice gift you gave should exonerate you of all guilt. You will want people at the wedding who genuinely care about you and your family, not casual acquaintances to whom you owe a favor.

My parents, rest their souls, were notorious for this tit-for-tat philosophy, as are much of their generation. It was a matter of "face" to show that you could return an invitation in kind. I remember having people at my wedding that I had to be introduced to, and being irate that inviting these folks caused many of my friends to be bumped from the list. Because my parents funded the entire wedding (I was only twenty and had just graduated college), their wishes took precedence over mine and my future husband's. To this day I resent that they took such control of the event. Don't do this to your child. Their friends are more important than any acquaintances to whom you feel obligated.

Rich folks

It's natural to want the most for our children—the best gifts, expensive china and silver, and lots of envelopes stuffed with money and checks. But it's wrong to invite specific people just because you know they will give a substantial gift. The bride and groom are neither beggars nor paupers. They are celebrating an event. Although a gift is accepted as a tribute to help them get started on their lives, it should not be criteria for an invitation. A related fallacy is to count on cash gifts to help pay for the wedding. Invite guests because they truly care about your family and the couple to be wed, and omit those others who are looking for another party to attend.

The "If I invite so and so, I must invite x" syndrome

It's easy to get caught up in guilt when planning your guest list. Are you contemplating inviting friends of friends so your buddies will have people to sit with? Think about each guest and determine his or her need to be there. If the relationship is casual and of no importance to the bride, groom, and primary sets of parents, there's no need to foot the expense for a costly dinner.

The sin of omission

When figuring dinner counts, don't forget to add in yourselves, the wedding party, and the participating vendors. You'll likely invite the minister and his wife to the reception. The photographer, videographer, DJ or band, and any assistants will need dinners, as well.

Create a final list

Even if our couple opts for e-invitations, the necessity of having a written listing of the guest list remains. A spreadsheet works well for keeping track of your guest list. Create one on computer or on lined paper, and list all the contact information for each guest. Ultimately, this will become your checklist for attendance. Set up your list so you can easily find a name. I found groupings of families and friends were more manageable than an alphabetical listing, but you may feel otherwise. List the bride's relatives and friends, the groom's relatives and friends, and then the service vendors in attendance. If the total guest list exceeds your original estimate, don't be appalled. Every tree gets new leaves.

Now, let's put some realism in the process, and calm you down a bit. The law of averages deems that 20 to 25 percent of the people you invite will return a "no." Go through the invitation list and draw a pencil line through those who aren't likely to attend because they live far away, have another known commitment that day, or are sick or otherwise incapacitated. You will still extend invitations to these folks, because they may surprise you and respond with a "yes," or they will be offended if they aren't included. Retotal this column. Use this estimate of actual attendees (versus total invites) as a revised head count and plan accordingly.

Etiquette books approve creating primary and backup guest lists. The backup list might be guests who you'd like to include, but can't accommodate if everyone on the primary list accepts. Be sure to send the first mailing out early enough, about ten to twelve weeks before the wedding, to allow backup invitations to go out no later than five weeks before the wedding. Again, use caution in doing this to avoid having a guest feel like a second fiddle. Word gets out quickly, and like the bridal shower guest who was offended by receiving a thank-you note weeks after others, applying two sets of criteria to your guest list can be risky.

Dear Joy,

I'm going to look like a cow at my child's wedding. Do you know a speed diet?

CHAPTER 11

Attiring

A T FIRST IT SEEMS THAT picking out the clothes to be worn at the wedding is the fun part, like receiving a gift after the hassle of getting the reception and guest list coordinated. You and your daughter have been reading bridal magazines and dog-earring pages since that ring first flashed on her finger. Even if the wedding will be a simple affair, what will be worn is significant. It will remain indelibly printed on photos and in your minds for all time—or, at least, for the length of the marriage.

What we wear at a wedding is more than clothing; we wear our insides on the outside. Our choice of attire defines who we are by allowing us to express ourselves outwardly. In addition to choosing what we like, we will also consider how our clothing will fit into the kind of ceremony and reception we plan. For example, nautical attire—casual red, white, and blue—is a natural choice for a shipboard ceremony, while country-style wear in natural earth tones may suit a ceremony held on a mountaintop.

You may see inappropriate clothing at a wedding, but if it is in concert with the wedding theme, is it wrong? In certain situations anything goes, as long as it isn't indecent. I've seen bridal bathing suits advertised for casual weddings at beach resorts, grass skirts and leis for weddings in Hawaii, and costumes for a Disney wedding or one held on Halloween. Oddball attire may not agree with your concept of the perfect wedding dress, but so what? Pick out your mask and wear it proudly. You *do* want to be part of the rest of your child's life, don't you?

Okay, so you lucked out

Tradition always feels right because it has been done over and over. The worst fear we have is not being in compliance with it. Suppose your bride and groom are "traditional." Your daughter will wear a white gown and veil and her groom will be dressed in formal attire. There will be bridesmaids and groomsmen and bouquets and that long white strip of cloth lining the aisle. You are comfortable with this because it is normal. All fear of disapproval falls away, leaving you free to shop for your attire in bridal shops and fancy boutiques instead of consignment stores, flea markets, funky catalogs, or costume shops. Hooray. You won this round.

You can already picture her dress, the bridesmaids, and yours. She'll wear white, of course, virginal white. But she wants the bridesmaids in black. Black at a wedding? Isn't that supposed to bring bad luck? Maybe she'll change her mind. There goes another rule by the wayside.

> *Marry in white, you have chosen right.*
> *Marry in grey, you will go far away.*
> *Marry in black, you'll wish yourself back.*
> *Marry in red, you'll wish yourself dead.*
> *Married in green, ashamed to be seen.*
> *Married in blue, you will always be true.*
> *Married in yellow, ashamed of your fellow.*
> *Married in pearl, you will live in a whirl.*
> *Married in brown, you will live in the town.*
> *Married in pink, your spirit will sink.*[25]

Certain colors no longer carry the stigmas they did in olden days, nor those imposed in more modern times. In my youth, guests weren't supposed to wear white or black to a wedding—white so they wouldn't compete with the bride, and black because it was reserved for funerals. With the popularity of evening weddings, the tendency toward sophistication has upped the color black from funereal to dressy. I've seen wedding photos with the bride and her bridesmaids attired in white. My first impression? Marshmallows with faces. But to each her own. White is more accepted for guests than in the past, especially in the summertime.

The bride and her entourage

The trauma of finding suitable attire for the wedding has just begun, because the bride and bridesmaids will continue the search *ad nauseum*. They share tips and titter about dresses that might work, and take multiple car trips to try them on and make comments. The bride will seldom travel without an entourage, which will be at least one or more bridesmaids, and you (if you were lucky enough to have been invited). I was thrilled when my future daughter-in-law asked me to go gown shopping with her, as this is often an honor reserved for the mother.

Gown hunt

Shop early! Most bridal shops, depending on the particular shop and designer, suggest gowns be chosen and ordered about six to eight months before the wedding to ensure the dress or dresses will arrive so they can be custom fit and ready on time. The search begins soon after the wedding date is chosen.

Beware of the bait and switch technique. In my Linda's case, the shop advertising a gown pictured in a bridal magazine didn't carry the exact model. The saleswoman was quick to bring us one she claimed was similar. When Linda tried on the gown, we gasped at its simple elegance. The dress fit her body as if it had been custom-made for her. Then, we checked the price tag. $2,000! My husband refused to pay that much, and Linda whined for the dress—her earlier, cheapo choice long forgotten. We settled on paying for half, plus the veil, which totaled what we had contributed for our first daughter's dress. To prevent hard feelings, a parent learns to keep things on par within a family.

Once your daughter or upcoming daughter-in-law finds a dress, it's smart business to compare pricing amongst the various shops and outlets. We were able to obtain the same dress for a couple of hundred dollars less by calling around and bargaining with local shop owners. To do this you'll need to know the manufacturer and model number, which you can copy off the dress tag. Ads in bridal magazines often provide listings of stores carrying their products, and you can also obtain this info via web searches. There are pros and cons of dealing with mail order companies and outlets. Avoid pitfalls and scams by consulting experts and by checking out wedding-oriented web sites.

If you plan to buy gowns locally, it makes sense to choose a bridal shop over a boutique. A bridal shop is equipped to handle wedding wear and will help match up the associated undergarments, shoes, and headwear to the dresses chosen by the bride and her attendants. Don't overlook having the bride's gown custom-made. Finding a good dressmaker is often done by word-of-mouth. A woman in our area designed and made gowns in her home; she created a custom look for a friend's daughter at a reasonable cost. The way this usually works is that you provide the materials and select the pattern or design, and the seamstress or tailor will provide the skill and make certain the dress fits properly.

Bridesmaids

The decision about attendants' wear will be made between the bride and her maids or matrons. A bridal shop will do all the coordination necessary to see that the gowns arrive and are fitted in time for the wedding—as long as they are provided the size information and deposit money when asked for. Money? This is one time when you don't need to think about it or spend it, unless you have other daughters in the wedding party. The commitment of being a bridesmaid means paying for one's own gown and all the trappings.

It's easy to get caught up in the hunt and make a few mistakes that could botch up the end result. As the older but wiser member of the entourage, caution the "girls" to order dresses from the same location to be sure the colors are uniform, as dye lots can vary. If the dresses are being custom made, ditto for the fabric. When distance is involved and a bridesmaid can't be fitted by the shop chosen, it's common to have her send her measurements to the shop. Be sure this bridesmaid has them taken correctly by a professional dressmaker in her area to avoid having the wrong size come in at the eleventh hour. A too-large dress can usually be altered, but one that's several sizes too small may be hopeless.

The search goes on . . .

It's fun being in the midst of all their chatter and decision-making, but sometimes you feel like the wise old owl. Of course, your daughter is young and beautiful and glows in everything she puts on. A bridesmaid or two might be with you, sharing the room, and pulling on dress after dress. They are stunning, they are gorgeous, and they are a size 6. "What about you, Mom?" your daughter asks. "What will you wear?"

You shuffle out to the showroom, riffle through the mother-of-the-bride rack, pull out a few size 12s, and then sneak off to a dressing room, alone. After witnessing all that model-like beauty, you feel like a fat, frump cow and nothing you try on seems to change that. You'll go another time, you tell yourself, and put off trying to cram that big butt, those sagging breasts, and your pear-shaped midsection into a flattering dress. You duck out of the dressing room and outright lie to your daughter that you didn't see anything you liked. She buys your story and leaves the subject be, for now.

They're finished, so you all go off to lunch, just what you need, and rehash the gown session. You liked them all, but she's fussy. Like selecting a Christmas tree from a crowded lot, there may be many that are suitable, but only one that's perfect. It's hard for you to tell, you cried over them all, and when she put on the matching veils it was hell. No mother should have to go through this emotion. It brings you back to your wedding, how you looked.

Were you as beautiful as your daughter is now?

When you arrive home, you go to the bookcase or dig through a carton in the basement and pull out your old wedding album. Curled up in a comfortable chair, you page through it, reminiscing. There were your parents; they are gone now. Your husband looked thinner and he had all his hair. But you like him better now. He's softer and more comfortable and you still get goose bumps when you look at him. You wonder what your son-in-law will look like when he's older.

It was a summer wedding so you chose daisies for your bridesmaids. They carried them in straw baskets and wore big-brimmed hats. Their dresses were sage green. And you, there was that fairy tale gown you had to have. It was worth every penny your parents spent on it—and you never did shorten it, dye it, and wear it again. You were married so young, barely out of school. Look at that tiny waist. Your hair was dark like your daughter's is now. You hadn't realized how much she looks like you.

You carefully close the album and hug it to you. Instead of replacing it in the carton, you take it to your bedroom and tuck it in your lingerie drawer. You spot yourself in the dresser mirror and push your face close, pulling at a few wrinkles to see what you looked like without them. You're not so perfect anymore, but you like your lived-in look. You run a comb through your hair, layer on a fresh coat of lipstick, and make an appointment for a facial.

Your dress, Madame

The mother of the groom does not have to wear beige. Once the bride has chosen a color scheme for the wedding and determined the formality of the bridesmaids' dresses, the mother of the bride traditionally chooses her gown. While it's not necessary that the groom's mother's dress match, it should neither clash nor be more formal than that of the bride's mother. That said, let's get you attired.

With so few occasions that allow us to dress up, we look forward to this with a mix of the excitement and trepidation of a first date. We diet and sign up for a gym membership to remold our bodies to the shape of that slinky dress we've had waiting in our closets for such an occasion, only to find it's outdated and curves in the wrong places. So we must have a new outfit—dress, shoes, and underwear—in roomier sizes.

Mother's dresses found in bridal shops seem to have the concession on sequins and beads and often come with jackets, which I suppose are intended to add warmth to an aging body or help to cover it up. Avoid choosing a dress that's so bright colored or flashy that those viewing you will need to wear sunglasses. If you find one in the lot that you love, you're luckier than I was. I found bridal shop gowns over-done and over-priced. Because yours will be a one-of-a kind dress—you don't need to buy ten of a style to suit a gamut of sizes and shapes—you have the flexibility to shop in interesting boutiques and department stores.

Your dress, Madame, should fit as if were custom-made for you, but not so snugly that you won't be able to zip it, should your stomach bloat the day of the ceremony. I spent an uncomfortable day in the purple gown that I had altered to show off my figure when my stomach popped out like a Jack-in-the-Box. At our age, stomachs bloat for all kinds of reasons; mine was water retention, yours may be gaseous from stress. Gratefully, my dress had a matching jacket, which I wore all day to hide the excess bulge.

Alterations

Bridal shops will order you the closest size, with plans to alter the dress to suit your figure. The problem is not girth, but height. It's hard to stretch or shrink specific parts of a dress without affecting the dress style. For a long-waisted person, a tailor alters the dress by lowering the curve of the waistline; but if you are petite or short-waisted, like I am, you're in trouble.

Being short-waisted means that the midriff area of a standard size dress will bubble with excess fabric, because the waistline wants to ride on your hip. The result is matronly. Dressmakers attempt to fix this problem by either raising the shoulders, which also lifts up the bust line of the dress (I don't know about you, but my breasts aren't that high any longer) or redoing the darts and seams around the midriff and waist. The result is seldom perfect. If you are not a standard size, shop at a store that carries formal wear in petite sizes or have your dress custom-made. The same $800 dress at a bridal shop can likely be recreated by a talented seamstress for much less, and the quality will be much better.

I've also noticed that the workmanship and fabric of some bridal store gowns is shoddy, as if they know the dress will only be worn once. Shoddy, but twice the price of department store gowns. We all think we'll wear a dress again; it's impractical not to. But, I tell you, I've three dresses in my closet that I've worn once because they never seem suited to another occasion. And I won't get into the extensive collection of old prom gowns and used bridesmaid dresses I've acquired from my daughters' events.

Men's stuff

Most of the hubbub over a wedding revolves around the bride: the chain of wedding events and the look of the wedding party—what she wears and how lovely she is. It's almost a reverse double standard, because we sometimes forget about the groom and groomsmen. What will they wear? Why aren't we making such a fuss about them? Is it because men's clothes tend to be boring? The selection of groom and usher attire isn't as flexible and fun for a formal wedding as it might be for a theme or destination wedding.

But, let's stick to traditional wedding garb, because formal garments require more planning and decorum. Few young men own a tuxedo, unless they are in the funeral business or work as paid escorts. Tuxedo rental joints are the male equivalent to bridal salons. There is little fluff surrounding male attire, because tuxedos are usually rented, not purchased. They don't need to be ordered much sooner than two weeks prior to the wedding.

As with any prewedding activity, there's a certain excitement about suiting up the men. The bride and groom will have already decided on the style and color of the tuxes, but will want to coordinate the accessories with the colors in the wedding. Although black tuxes are standard, a summer wedding may feature white ones, and certain climates and cultures may call for a colored tux. Depending on the degree of formality, the styling could be jacket-and-slacks co-ordinates, dark suits, or tails. Add a touch of whimsy with colorfully patterned vests, bow ties, and cummerbunds.

Making certain all the men provide the rental store their measurements beforehand bears monitoring. Typically, the groom handles this. Once done, the men simply stop in a few days before the wedding for a fitting, and then pick up the garments in time for the event. Unlike bridal wear, the tuxes need to be returned to the shop in a timely fashion. Arrange to have a local groomsman collect and return the goods on the first working day after the wedding.

Father of the bride or groom

Dad's tuxedo doesn't need to match those of the wedding party, but it shouldn't scream, "civil war." If your husband has an old tux that still fits him lingering in the closet, take a look at it. It might be dated. Compare the shape of the lapels, the amount of shoulder padding and the style to those selected for the wedding. It would be embarrassing to have Dad look as if he walked out of the dark ages.

It's okay to have some fun with the accessories, once the serious part of the wedding is past. My husband found a reversible vest, a sedate white on one side with a Mickey Mouse print on the other. He kept the matching Mickey Mouse bow tie in his pocket, and did the old switcheroo for the reception. It got a good laugh out of everyone, and he loved the attention.

Dude-ing up loved ones

Getting the wedding party members' outfits set is not the only the hurdle. The mother in you deems that you attend to other special people in your life who need assistance in looking their best. These may be sons or daughters who will not be in the wedding party or grandparents and elderly relatives who are special to you. Don't wait until the last minute to discover they have nothing to wear that fits them, looks nice on them, or suits the occasion.

Other sons or daughters

It's common to have sons or daughters who are not part of the wedding party. No matter what their ages or sexes, it's important to attend to their outfits, as well. Make special efforts to include them in the attire planning. If you can afford it, buy them something new in which they can enjoy parading around in at the wedding. This isn't always as easy as it sounds. Teenagers in particular have a propensity not to conform.

Shaved heads, Kool-Aid dyed hair in brilliant rainbow colors, and hip-hop, funky, or suggestive clothing will make your child a sore thumb. You might have become accustomed to this by now, but older guests will mutter and point. Use whatever means you can devise to prevent him or her from becoming a spectacle. I've found bribery works. Elicit the assistance of someone he or she respects—the bride, groom, or a youthful friend—to, just this once, wear the outfit you've helped select, and to keep hair tamed to an acceptable color or style.

Grandparents

Grandma and Grandpa are always special. I love to see older folks at weddings. They have so few opportunities to dress up. The thrill of buying something new and looking pretty or handsome can bring that wonderful sparkle of youth back into their eyes. Work with your elderly loved ones on this. You will likely need to take them shopping. While they may have a perfectly appropriate dress or suit hanging in their closet, it may need to be cleaned and pressed to look fresh, or you may need to assist them in buying a new one.

If they are frail, and shopping is too exhausting for them, bring the store to them. Select from the rack a few dresses or suits in their sizes and ask the sales clerk if you might take the items home for approval. Most shops will be understanding if you explain the circumstances. "Buy" the clothes with a charge card and with the store's agreement that you may return unsuitable items.

While you are nosing around in Grandma or Grandpa's closet, check out their shoe wardrobe. Older folks have the most beat-up shoes. Bunions and foot problems increase with age, and there's a tendency to retain old comfortable shoes and to wear them everywhere. Find out their favorite brands and styles and help them select a new pair that will work with the dress or suit they will wear to the wedding.

Clothes for related events

While you are shopping, keep an eye out for clothes that will be appropriate for you and your family to wear to events surrounding the wedding. You'll need dinner clothes for the rehearsal dinner, and nice outfits for the shower, luncheons, or other parties. By planning these outfits in advance, you will eliminate the frustration of spending time in a too-tight dress with matching shoes that needed replacing long ago. Try everything on for fit, comfort, and style at least a month in advance, so you'll have time to lose weight or replace the parts of the outfit that don't work.

Fluffing

Hair and makeup are individual, yet on a festive occasion such as this, it's tempting to get creative—a new style, new makeup. Part of the wedding fluff is for the bride to make several visits to her favorite salon to test out hairdos for the wedding day. Usually, the headpiece she will wear is brought to the salon visit, so it can be incorporated into the "do." Upsweeps are considered very formal, and will most easily stay in place all day. Bridal shops often recommend them, as do hairdressers.

My advice to you all is don't be conned into a hairdo that you are not comfortable with. If you never wear your hair up because you are self-conscious about your Ross Perot ears or of a birthmark on the nape of your neck, this is not the time to do it. Wear the style that feels like "you."

Make salon appointments for the attendants several months in advance. Part of the fun is doing this as a group. The salon will need to carve out time and space, as well as enough stylists and manicurists to attend to your needs. We asked our favorite hairdresser to come to the house and blow dry and style the bride's and bridesmaids' hair on the morning of Linda's wedding. This worked out beautifully, and the girls could sit around and advise each other. I paid the hairdo bills, and each girl took care of her own tip.

Manicures and pedicures are typically done the day before the wedding, and often followed by a bridesmaids' lunch—a sandwich at a local restaurant will do or you can prepare something simple back at the house. The day will be busy, because there is a rehearsal dinner at night, the prelude to the event and the start of the festivities. Hair and makeup are styled the day of the wedding—very early for a late morning or afternoon ceremony—so they will look fresh. Headpieces are set in place at this time, as well. It's common to see a bride running last-minute errands wearing her veil and a pair of jeans.

Set it and forget it

One of the worst problems we women face on a day such as this, when we risk being photographed at every turn, is keeping our hair and makeup intact. The best solution for hair is to resign yourself to being helmet head for the day. Tease and spray hair so that it will not move, even in a stiff wind, and don't worry about how it feels. No one that you care about will be running their fingers through it. Your hair may feel like it belongs on someone else's head, but it's looks that count. And you'll enjoy having your hair look consistently good all day without having to redo or fuss with it.

For makeup, do your best job, and then set it with a light dusting of powder. If you keep your hands away from your face and try not to bite your lips, your makeup will stay pretty much intact. That doesn't take into account the emotional aspects, though. No doubt you will be sobbing through the ceremony and emerge with a red, runny nose and weepy eyes dripping streaks of mascara. There is makeup designed to withstand a day at the beach; certainly it will help for this occasion. Be smart when you try new products and play with them in advance of the big day. Note how well they wear and how often, if ever, they require touchup. Be certain your skin isn't sensitive to an ingredient in a product, lest you develop a rash, itchy eyes, or worse when you want to look your best.

Other loved ones

When you are making your appointment with the hairdresser for your wedding hairdos and manicures, remind your mother and others you care about to make theirs, as well. If they require transportation, drive them yourself or solicit another family member to take them.

Relatives or future in-laws coming in from out of town may need help finding last-minute services. Ask what they will require in advance of their visit. After all, if they are traveling across country to see your child prance down the aisle, this is the least you can do for them. If they are not familiar with the area, locate shopping malls, drugstores, hairdressers, and barbers in the area where they will be staying and provide them names and phone numbers so they can arrange appointments. If they do not have a car available, either loan them one or advise them where to rent one.

Dear Joy,

I love a party, but do I have to plan all of them?

CHAPTER 12

Presents and More Parties

T HE ENTIRE WEDDING PROCESS IS a cause for celebration, beginning with the engagement. A bridal shower or stag party and a rehearsal dinner are integral, but there could be other parties to plan, as well. You may host an arrival supper or hotel hospitality room for out-of-town relatives and friends, or decide to follow the wedding with an after-party or a next-day brunch. Your decisions will depend on space availability, finances, and timing. Use your judgment, based on the style of wedding and the number and types of guests invited, as to what will work best for you all.

Gifting

If your young couple hasn't already done so, encourage them to set up a gift registry. This will help prevent them from receiving items they don't need or care for, and make it easier for guests who haven't something specific in mind to choose a gift. Couples often sign up for multiple registries—anywhere from Crate & Barrel and Bed Bath & Beyond to Home Depot or Wal-Mart. Many of these stores are accessible via the internet, making it easy to keep track of gift orders and to arrange shipping, and are often linked to the couple's website.

The downside of this magical process is that some people will want to stick to the old-fashioned means of selecting a gift. Once a wedding is in the offing, your phone will start buzzing with questions from relatives and friends who have not yet accepted the digital age. What does the couple *really* need? What colors are they using in the bathroom, bedroom, and kitchen? Where are they registered?

We all know that requesting an item doesn't guarantee they'll get it. Reasonably priced items will be selected first. Costly selections may not be purchased, unless several guests decide to go in together to buy them. A group of relatives chipped in toward buying my son and his wife the barbecue grill they wanted.

You can help by offering guidance and advice. Suggest that your couple specify brands, catalog numbers, and UPC codes, especially in the case of small appliances, to be sure they won't have to trek back to the store to make an exchange or return. Talk about quality, number and types of linens they'll need, and help them think through whether or not an item is necessary. A 20-cup coffee urn, for example, that may be needed once every three years can certainly be rented, rather than collect dust and hog precious pantry space.

Be tactful with your suggestions, and perhaps they will listen. While there is certainly nothing wrong with starting a life with kitchen-quality dishes—mine came from the supermarket, if your couple has a chance to go for the brass ring, why not?

My daughter-law hadn't planned to register for the "good stuff." She felt their life was so casual they would never use it.

"Honey," I told her, "if you don't ask for these goodies now, you won't get another chance. Once you are married and have begun your family, you'll l never want to part with the money to indulge yourselves. Do it now and you'll never have to say you're sorry."

I know Lois loves her fine china, now. We've enjoyed many a festive dinner on its platters.

If your daughter is living at home or if your address is on the gift registration list for convenience, you might be the recipient of lots of packages in the interim between the engagement and the ceremony. You can't open them (maybe shake them and note who sent them) because they are not yours. Find a place to store the boxes until the couple can deal with them. With the exception of shower presents, which are usually brought and opened at the event, wedding packages often come by parcel post or U.S. mail. A few guests will bring wrapped gifts to the ceremony, which you (the collective you) will need to pack up and take home at the end of a long day. Checks or monetary gifts are usually placed in the hands of the bride or groom at the ceremony, although some may come tucked in a wedding congrats card by mail.

> *The concept of wedding gift-giving has ancient origins, beginning with the dowry, which was a payoff for the groom to take a daughter off one's hands. Woe to the lass who fell in love with a guy that didn't meet Dad's approval, for there would be no dowry. Sometimes her friends would get together and shower her with enough loot to make a dowry so she could marry the guy of her choice. It is also said that the practice of showering the bride began in Holland, about 1890. The bride's friends put small gifts inside a parasol and opened it over the bride's head so that the presents would "shower" over her to make her life of matrimony comfortable. (Let's hope those gifts were light enough not to do permanent injury.) While we no longer dump packages over a prospective bride's head, gifting has remained an integral part of the wedding process.*[26]

Showering

Wedding gifts may trickle in once invitations have been issued, but the bride will be deluged at her bridal showers. While gifts may be chosen from the couple's registry, it's common to have a theme shower requesting a particular type of item, such as lingerie, luggage, or outfitting an area of the couple's new home. Theme showers work particularly well for small groups and secondary showers. For a kitchen shower, I was asked to submit a favorite recipe along with my gift. There are also showers centered on the boudoir or the bath, as well as those for house and yard supplies. Be sure to indicate the type of shower you are giving in the invitation along with any helpful information, such as the color scheme of the room, decorating style—contemporary, country, or traditional; or for lingerie, the bride's sizes.

It's a shame that bridal showers have grown into such monsters. What happened to those intimate at-home parties we used to put on? I'll always treasure the memories of the small gatherings that were once the norm, consisting of practical gifts and lots of laughs. In some areas of the country, this simplicity may still exist, but in the Northeast U.S.A. a typical bridal shower is now an orchestrated affair with the couple registering for a home-load of gifts. Sure, you'll attend the afternoon tea at a home, but don't be surprised if it's catered. Women work, and have less time to spend fussing over preparing elaborate party dishes for a crowd or scrubbing down the house for company. Some prefer to hire in help to handle the party at home, or to have the function at a hall or restaurant—where someone else can do the dishes and sweep up afterward.

Who gives it?

Anyone can give a shower except the mother of the bride, according to etiquette books. Why? Because it implies a plea for gifts. Give me a break! Of course it's a plea for gifts. The purpose of a bridal shower is to give the couple a leg up on supplies needed for their home such as, linens, dinnerware, bedding, and a trousseau. While bridesmaids aren't directly responsible for giving the shower, it's common for them to feel the need to host one, unless other friends or relatives of the bride and groom step up to the plate.

In the good old days, it was easy to say, "Sure I'll give so and so a shower," because it could be done cheaply and simply at home. With today's need for extravaganzas, fewer offers to host come forth from relatives and friends, often leaving the shower arrangements to the bride's parents and the maid of honor. With all the other costs involved in being a member of the wedding party, it borders on friendship abuse to expect the bridesmaids to also pay for a shindig involving substantial food and drink and a large group of guests.

The reality is the bride's family usually shells out the bucks for the food and many of the trimmings for affairs intended to include relatives and friends of both parents, thus removing the burden of expense from the bridesmaids. If you will be paying for a formal shower for your daughter, be a silent partner. Work with the maid or matron of honor and the rest of the women in the party, but take a back seat to the kudos. Let them plan the theme, write out the invitations, and reap the honors of being hostesses. They'll decorate, create a special chair for your daughter to sit in, help her open and show off gifts, and flutter around her like mother hens. (Hey, maybe they'll even stick bows in paper plates for a mock bridal bouquet. It's tradition, you know.) All that extra attention they pay your daughter won't cost you a penny. And, your daughter will be spoiled, as she should be, on her special day.

If the groom's family is large, his parents may offer to help pay for part of the affair. My future daughter-in-law's parents were unable to give her a shower, and my son was concerned. I colluded with a longtime family friend, who offered her home and, with the help of the bridesmaids, all the trappings including the Irish lace tablecloth and hand-painted favors. I provided the cake, most of the food, and my able-bodied assistance in setting up for the party. Both our names went on the invite. Was this proper? Who cares? My daughter-in-law was totally surprised and thrilled. She received lots of wonderful gifts, the sun was shining, the wine was flowing—and my son was smiling.

Where and how

No need to worry much about what type of shower to have, because your child will have already thought it through. It's part of the dream. We love our children and do the best we can to help their dreams become reality, but sometimes the money isn't there. There are no rules, remember? If your son or daughter's concept of a prenuptial party doesn't jive with your pocketbook, lay out what you can afford and put it to them to decide if they will shrink the party or toss in some of their own funds to have it their way.

My Mary wanted something unusual, so we arranged with a playscape in town to rent one of their party rooms. We mimicked a children's birthday party, with gourmet pizzas, cake, and party bags. Afterwards, the "girls" took turns going down the big slide in the playscape. Linda wanted to have her shower at home, but with a headcount of sixty, it was hard to keep it simple. Understand that at a comprehensive shower, the guests will number half of the wedding invites, so the size of the shower will be in proportion to the size of the wedding. Our sunken living room became the event's arena. By closely spacing rented chairs, we were able to squeeze in every person.

My alternatives were to swelter over preparing and serving gargantuan portions of food or to solicit contributions from relatives and friends. I took the high road and hired a catering service. The kitchen was a bustle of folks I didn't know, but the food that came pumping out of it was marvelous. Still, I found myself running back and forth making sure the caterer knew when to do what. The house roared with activity. I had such a migraine that day.

A current idea is to put on a Jack and Jill Party in lieu of a shower. Can you guess what that implies? You've got it! It means you'll be holding the equivalent guest count of a wedding reception as a shower, because instead of entertaining just the women, you've got the men too. Men eat more, drink more, and are almost as messy. Here, the shower is honoring both the bride and groom—but keep in mind that a Jack and Jill Party won't replace the stag.

It takes more to entertain people these days, and the simplicity of the traditional shower is becoming more complex. Some new ideas have surfaced that will work well for showers involving small groups of people. An interactive shower entails group participation in a sport or project, such as scrap-booking, ending with a casual meal or snacks. With an entertainment-oriented shower, everyone chips in towards tickets to a show or event, and then goes out for a drink or dessert afterwards. At a progressive dinner shower, the host transports the shower guests in a mini-van or hired bus to a different restaurant or home for each course. Presents are sent ahead to the last stop.

Don't be tacky

In some instances, a bride is given several showers. Her co-workers at the office might put one on, her bridesmaids may do one with intimate friends; but the mother lode is the shower the parents want, which includes relatives, neighbors, and friends of the family—the *older* folks. These are the people who will give place settings of china, crystal, flatware, and large sums of money. It goes back to our general invitation process. Be sure anyone included in the affair is there because they should be, and not for financial gain. Keep in mind when planning mini events, such as office showers, that it is the height of rudeness to ask a person who will not be invited to the wedding to contribute toward or to purchase a shower gift.

Gifts are expected at a shower, yet it's tacky to dictate to guests what those gifts should be and how they should be given. It's crass to state blatantly the couple's preference for money in the invitation, even if this is the case; but if you are asked what the couple needs, use this opening to explain that they would prefer a gift certificate or money.

While we're on the subject of gifts, I'm wondering how many of you have been forced to sit with a cup of punch at a shower while the bride opens every single gift? This is fine for an intimate shower, where the gift can be passed around or easily ogled, but I feel enduring the procedure for fifty gifts or more borders on guest abuse. In a large room, it's hard to see the gifts, let alone hear who sent them. Once the meal or refreshment has been served, it would be a kindness to announce the opening of gifts, and then give guests the option of staying or leaving. Another thought is to suggest gifts be sent in advance so they can be pre-opened and displayed at the shower.

Surprise!

The attempt to surprise the bride still exists, and works fine for intimate showers. For a larger, more formal shower, it is kinder to reduce the bride-to-be's stress about walking into a home or restaurant only to be shouted at and feted while wearing no makeup, her crappiest clothes, and having a bad hair day. A shower is usually held a couple of months before the wedding, so the bride expects something to happen within that time. She lives on the edge each time she walks in a room. Why put her through all this just so you can blab about how shocked she was? My sister-in-law broke out in hives at her shower, and they live on in all the photos we took.

But surprise is half the fun, you say? Righto. But it isn't always necessary to go all the way. We held Mary's shower in Connecticut, but because she lived in New Jersey at the time, it needed to be coordinated with her visit. We told her when it was scheduled, but not where or what. Her dad and I blindfolded her, tucked her in the car, and drove to the playscape. We kept her blindfolded until we reached the room. She was surprised without being embarrassed. She'd done her hair and makeup and wore a carefully selected outfit.

Back at the house

A party is never over when it's over. Folks who have traveled a long distance to attend and are overnighting in the area will want to hang around. Most showers are daytime events; this means you may be hauling out food for supper. Leftovers from the party work well, as do a cold cut platter, rolls, and salads preordered from the deli. Otherwise, there's always take-out or delivery. An after-shower party doesn't need to be fancy; it's often a let-your-hair-down event that rounds out the day. While we were "showering" at the playscape, the guys were at our home watching the ball game and salivating for the leftovers. We filled an ice chest with beer, wine, and soft drinks and set out the leftover pizza and cake on the kitchen counter, along with paper plates and forks. The girls changed to sweats and lolled about with glasses of wine and talked wedding stuff, while the men chatted about their jobs.

The stag party

The stag or bachelor party has long been considered a final fling for the groom. Ancient Spartan solders were the first to hold what has become known as stag parties. The groom would feast with his male friends on the night before his wedding as a way of saying goodbye to his carefree days and of pledging loyalty to his friends.[27] The tradition has been carried on through the years, and is often thought of as a rowdy event involving porn, strippers, and lap dancers.

While this may have once been the case, our men have matured. The average male now marries at about 26 years, so he hopefully has passed the drinking-and-partying-with-the-guys stage and is more settled and financially stable than his younger predecessors. The loyalty-to-friends portion of the rite remains, but the trend is towards well-organized, fun-filled parties and events planned with care and sensitivity. The newest bachelor parties reflect the groom's interests. The groom and his friends may go away on a fishing trip, charter a boat, arrange a golf weekend in Myrtle Beach, or fly to Las Vegas for a weekend of sunning and gambling. This isn't to say that they might not stop off at a strip club, but that the stag party has become more wholesome in concept.

As a mother, I am thrilled to know that no son of mine will be found lying sloppy drunk in an alley, but instead might be sleeping off a hangover in a nice, clean hotel room, alone.

From reading this, you no doubt have surmised that, like everything else, stags have become more structured and elaborate. Remember, every event has a range. There is no problem with best friends taking the groom out for a night of bowling and pizza or to hire a hall for a one-night affair. The best man and ushers are normally responsible for planning the agenda. An overnight excursion can become complicated when it involves transportation and lodging expenses. Some stags sell tickets to pay for the meal and a gift. In cases where money is needed to pull off the event, *cherchez la* dad. The father of the groom is indirectly involved, yet he may be funding the event, much the same as a mother supports the bridal shower effort.

Tips for stag parties

Smart stag planners will avoid having the celebration on the eve of the wedding for obvious reasons. It's a good idea to time the party a week, or even a month, before the wedding. Keep the guest list manageable and avoid offering casual or open-ended invitations that allow guests to bring friends. This will expand the event beyond control and overshadow the essence of the stag, sharing a special time with good buddies.

Decide on the location of the event, and be certain it is large enough to accommodate the invited guests. It's common to rent a hall for large parties. Consider that you will need to arrange for seating, linens, dinnerware, and enough food to feed the gang. It wouldn't be a party without liquor. Decide if you will limit the party to beer, wine, and soft drinks or if hard liquor will be offered. Arrange for some sort of food, no matter how casual the event. Pizza is fine, or have the event catered.

Smut is out and clean fun is in. Never assume a groom wants female entertainment. Most modern males are responsible and don't care to do anything they might not normally do at a party, or to upset their fiancés. Always remember that whatever happens, the bride *will* find out and the groom *will* be in deep trouble.

And lastly, ensure guests arrive home safely. Commission a non-drinking driver to shuttle people home from the party or hire a limo or bus.

As a mom, you're totally bypassed for your son's stag party (and may be grateful for that). He's told you about his tux, but you weren't included in the visit to pick it out. Even your husband didn't take part in that one. You feel useless, like a limp arm on an active body. So, you throw yourself into planning the rehearsal dinner. That's as close to the wedding as you can get. If it's a small wedding, a rehearsal dinner is no big event to handle; but if the party is large, you're in heaven. You get to send out fancy invites that you pick yourself, make up a seating plan, and select decorations for the table. You control this event and even make final decisions over whom to invite. Doing something helps defray those bouts of uselessness and unimportance that have left you feeling guilty. You don't dare tell anyone. Everyone surmises you're bustling like a busy bee getting ready for the wedding, when in fact you're calm, relaxed and have extra time on your hands—the time you took off work to get ready that you don't even need.

Rehearsal dinner

Planning a rehearsal dinner seems like child's play as compared to the reception. This function is intended for the actual wedding participants. While it is customary for the groom's parents to handle the expense and planning, it is not an obligation. The rehearsal dinner can be hosted by the bride's family, the parents of an attendant, or a relative or close friend. The degree of simplicity or formality of the rehearsal dinner will be in concert with the wedding that follows, as well as with the bank account of the persons hosting it. If you can't afford a formal dinner at a restaurant, offer a meal at your home. It can be a simple casserole, salad, and store-bought cake—just don't serve cheap wine.

Oftentimes, the wedding is held in the bride's hometown, which may not be where the groom and or his parents reside. It is naturally more complicated to arrange a dinner party in an unfamiliar place. I assume if you are the groom's mother that you are on speaking terms with the bride and her mom. Work with them to create a guest list so you will know the size of your group, and then ask for restaurant suggestions. If you are visiting or live nearby, stop by to speak with the banquet manager and obtain a menu, otherwise call and ask to have the information mailed, faxed, or e-mailed to you.

The basic guest list will consist of the wedding party, the immediate families of the bride and groom, and anyone singing, playing an instrument, or doing a reading at the ceremony. The officiant and his or her spouse, of course, should be on the invite list. Find out if there will be any close relatives or friends coming in from out of town who should be included. Understand that the guest list, like the wedding list, will grow. If you are not paying for an event (perhaps you are the mother of the bride), it's gracious to offer to fund additional meals caused by extra people you wish to include. Once you have a total list, send out invitations, as you would for any party. No formality needed, here. Handwrite the invitations, create them on your computer, or send out e-invitations.

Bridal luncheon

There are no rules for what is loosely called the bridal luncheon. As the mother of the bride you can leave the planning and execution of this event to your daughter. The purpose of this event is to give the bride a chance to spend time with her "maids" and to bestow thank-you gifts for their support. The bride personally selects and pays for these gifts; so, as a parent, your only obligation is to ooh and aah at her choices.

As with everything related to a wedding, this gathering can be elaborate and expensive or done on the cheap. Your daughter and her maids might go out drinking together, spend a day at the beach, plan the luncheon around a play or a movie, or spend a girl's weekend in New York City. Often the "luncheon" is held the day before the wedding to include out-of-town bridesmaids. When my daughters were married, we arranged group manicures and pedicures for all the bridesmaids at a local salon, and then treated everyone to lunch at a local restaurant afterwards—nothing fancy, a Friday's or a Ruby Tuesday's.

If money and time are tight, you might offer to put together a casual lunch at home—which can be sandwiches, pizza, salad, whatever. If this luncheon is held within a day of the wedding, it's wise to avoid offering spicy foods that might bring on halitosis or flatulence.

Hospitality room

For arriving out-of-town guests staying at a hotel, consider setting up a hospitality room or suite, where they can congregate and have a drink, snack, or buffet-style meal. If the preponderance of folks is from the groom's side, the groom's parents would take care of this arrangement and vice versa.

When my brother's daughter was married, having a hospitality room solved the problem of including a large number of extra people in the rehearsal dinner count. We all stopped by to greet everyone, afterwards. If you wish, you can extend the room reservation to include the wedding day and offer guests a continental breakfast. A two-day reservation will also provide a good place to gather after the wedding.

After-party

If your couple's wedding reception ends late afternoon, it's nice to continue the party elsewhere, perhaps by offering some sort of meal or drinks and snacks. The only rule, here, is that the invitation be extended to everyone attending the wedding reception. Years ago, when I was married, my parents invited everyone back to their house for more drinks and a buffet supper.

If you are too busy to take on this responsibility, perhaps a relative or close friend might offer to host or arrange such an event. Refreshments could be home-cooked, catered, or provided in a nearby restaurant. With this type of party you risk having an overwhelming response to your open invitation. Typically, you need to figure on family and close friends of the bride, guests staying overnight, and any others who you know won't pass up a chance for free food and drink.

With the popularity of the evening wedding, the after-party is a more a casual gathering of folks who want to stay on after the wait staff at the reception hall has cleared the tables and the DJ or band has packed up. While the majority of the guests will yawn and go home, close friends and relatives of the bride and groom are apt to stick around. The location might be anywhere comfortable that allows people to mingle, such as that hospitality room or a local watering hole. It's customary for the bride, groom, and wedding party to make an appearance, but they have no obligation to stay until the party fizzles out.

Morning-after get-togethers

You thought you could sit on your laurels and relax once the wedding day was over, didn't you? Sorry, but you have people who came in from Lord-knows-where and are still here. They sacrificed time and money just to be present at your son or daughter's wedding, which means they care about them. Give these folks a proper send-off.

If you have a large group staying at a hotel that includes a complimentary breakfast with the room, you might be off the financial hook. This was the case with my first daughter's wedding. Our family sat in the lobby enjoying coffee while we visited with friends and relatives as they straggled in. It was a nice way to spend some casual time with everyone before they departed for home. After one wedding, we had an impromptu bagel-and-cream cheese breakfast at our home for the wedding party and favorite relatives—whoever showed up or was around joined us. The bride and groom opened up wedding presents that had been brought to reception and landed at our home.

Pre-planning an official brunch comes with a new set of obligations, which means more work and more money. At this point, you are probably so numb to money outlays that you will hardly care. At an out-of-town wedding my husband and I attended, the bride and groom arranged to have a buffet breakfast set up in a private area of the hotel hosting the reception. With open seating, foods were available most of the morning, which allowed us to eat and to visit with other guests before we flew home.

Another alternative is to host a formal brunch in your home or that of a close friend or relative. Include time, location, and directions for your brunch in a separate invitation, which can be either be included with the wedding invitation or sent on its own.

Dear Joy,

Is this the fun part? I'm buried in minutia.
Help!

CHAPTER 13

The Countdown

IT'S INTERESTING HOW THIS WEDDING thing plays out. You spend the first month or two after the engagement running around setting up dates and places, and the last two months tying up loose ends and confirming things. As the big day neared, I carried an appointment book with me full of things that needed doing. This is a good time to review all your notes and files, confirm arrangements, and check on funds for final payments that will need to be made before the wedding.

With so many little things to remember, it's easy to become buried in the minutia of such tasks as hunting for chicken and cow stickers for the place cards at the wedding reception, or locating inexpensive baskets to fill for favors. I added a task to my list whenever it popped into my head, and took pleasure in crossing off those that were completed.

If you think about it, you'll realize that much of the running around is related to the reception. The venue will need to have a final guest count by a specified date; and one or two days before the wedding, whatever your contract specifies, you will need to drop off any table favors, photos, or special items you wish to have set out. And, oh yes, be prepared with a check for the final payment. All that done, you will feel as if a large burden has been lifted from you. More importantly, you'll realize that the wedding wheel has been set in motion and all you need to do is roll along with it.

Set up a prewedding agenda

The best way to reduce stress and make sure everything goes smoothly on the wedding day is to put together an agenda. It's easy to forget small things when so much is happening at once. Begin by making a list of everything that needs to be done. Put the tasks in order, assign times to them, and then delegate them to specific people. Make copies of your final schedule for those on your to-do list and highlight their tasks. Cell phones, text messaging, and e-mail are a Godsend during this hectic time for I-forgots and whatnots.

Wedding event schedule should include:

- Names and times of arrival for everyone involved
- Home phone, cell phone numbers for everyone involved
- Directions to sites
- Specifics for ceremony
- Time estimate for each activity
- Specific notes for each vendor
- Transportation info

Now, help your husband feel important by putting him in charge of the task list. There. You can relax and enjoy readying for the rehearsal dinner, and then the wedding the next day. Enjoy this special time surrounded by all those lovely young women or handsome men.

Guests

As you think through the day, consider the needs of your guests. If you have planned a "destination" or vacation-oriented wedding that requires guests to travel and stay at a resort hotel, you are under no obligation to pay airfare and accommodation costs. While it is a nice gesture, it is not necessary. Folks should attend because they want to, and part of their commitment is bearing any personal expenses. In special instances where you know a person can't come because of the expense, you may graciously offer to help. But understand this is your choice, your gift.

Do research good rates for airfare and accommodations and pass the information on to prospective guests. Take the time to investigate any hotels and flights you suggest. Cheaper isn't always best. It would be embarrassing to have Aunt Tilda subjected to a no-tell-motel that offered siesta stints to unmarried couples. Choose a hotel, motel, or inn you know is reputable or look for multi-starred ratings in travel books or on websites. And, can Gramps tolerate a flight that requires several connections? If you query airlines well in advance, you'll improve the chances of finding him a direct flight at a low cost. If you know he and Grandma are living on Social Security and that coming to the wedding will be a hardship, offer to buy their tickets so they can share this day with you.

Provide guests with as much travel and lodging information as you can, but leave it to them to choose the option that works best. For those living a good distance away, we included in the wedding invitation an insert listing nearby hotels, costs, and telephone numbers, as well as applicable flight or other travel information.

If a large number of people will be staying overnight in the area, it makes sense to locate a reasonably-priced hotel or motel that will reserve a block of rooms for your event. This enables all your guests to be together and makes it easier to visit with them and to transport them to wedding-related festivities. Avoid becoming tangled in handling reservations. You are not a hotel clerk and shouldn't take on the responsibility of pleasing everyone. Leave it to invitees to call in their own reservations, using their charge card numbers to hold them. At that time they can make special requests for a handicapped or non-smoking room, a king-sized bed, extra cots, or a crib.

Likewise, you needn't feel obligated to send fruit baskets or bottles of wine to their rooms or to give guests other presents for attending the wedding. It is nice, however, to provide sightseeing brochures for those who may be extending their stay, especially if there are tourist attractions in the area.

House guests

Think before you offer your home to guests. Can you comfortably accommodate them? Grandma may not be happy if relegated to a pull-out sofa and you might need to give up your bed to her. This is fine under normal circumstances, but as the mother of the bride or groom being ousted from your bedroom will definitely cramp your style. Once she's abed, you'll fear sneaking in to use the shower or to rummage through your drawers and closets for clothes and makeup. If you know your home will be a tight squeeze, make other arrangements for loved ones. Perhaps Grandma could stay at a nearby daughter's home, or with another relative who isn't directly involved in the wedding event. Understand your limits and don't stretch them too far. There will be enough stress to deal with without adding to it.

Transportation

Transportation to and from the various wedding events may also be a problem. If guests are staying in the same hotel, it will be easy for them to form a follow-the-leader entourage to reach the various events or to car pool. Provide clear directions for travel between sites, and be sure to include a cell phone number they can call for clarification. Even though you've provided detailed directions, it's easy enough to misinterpret them. We had an elderly uncle who was so confused by the directions that he and his wife arrived just as the bride and groom finalized their vows. To avoid such problems, take folks like these under your wing and arrange to have them ride with other guests.

Another issue is the drinking problem. Many of your guests will be driving home or back to a hotel afterwards, and you want them to arrive there safely and without incident. Set cards around the reception hall, on each table if you have a seating arrangement, with the name and phone number of a local cab company. A hotel may also offer shuttle service, if you request it.

Invitation returns

You tussle with whom you should or shouldn't invite to the wedding and argue over the costs. You sent out invitations using your final roster—with a few regrets—and then, the deed is done. All that awaits the collective you are the returns and your prayers that *everyone* won't say "yes." It's awful, but I can remember us checking response after response in hopes of a few "nos." We found that those who are certain they can attend usually respond at once. "Nos" and "wishy-washys" hang on to their invitations longer, as a reminder to send a gift.

After the first flood of returns, the remainder will trickle in. The best way to manage this process is for the recipient, who might be you or your daughter, to transfer the responses to the guest list. To avoid lapses, it's wise to hang on to the original responses as a cross check for accuracy, especially for a sit-down dinner with a seating plan and meal choices. Should you receive returns with names of additional guests, such as their children, added on, don't be bullied into adding these names to your already-too-long roster. Phone the person and tactfully explain that you cannot include extra people. If you make an exception for one person, others will expect the same courtesy.

Understand folks aren't always good about adhering to the RSVP dates on invitations. Maybe they forgot to look or lost track of time. Before they've realized it, they've missed the commit-by date. There always will be a handful of people you have yet to hear from. If your response is timed to within three weeks of the wedding, you can afford to give stragglers an extra week before you nudge them.

Assemble a "lagger list" composed of those who haven't responded. Divide it up amongst you, according to closeness to the person, and start phoning or e-mailing them. Ask bridesmaids and ushers to follow up with friends of the bride and groom, and future in-laws to check with their relatives. A few of my relatives thought they had already responded, but they hadn't. My phone call set the record straight. It would have been embarrassing for one of these dear ones to arrive at the reception hall and not have a place setting.

The X#*#@X seating chart

It's important to provide table assignments for guests for any type of meal, sit-down or buffet. This prevents confusion, bickering, seat-saving, and having a group that should sit together split up. Making up the required seating chart for the reception is a political nightmare for most families, especially large ones. It involves the input of at least four parties—the bride, groom, and their parents. The reception hall will normally provide a room layout sheet with numbered locations of the dining tables. All you do need to do is fill in the names of the people to be seated at each table.

Easier said than done.

We cut apart a list of attendees so we could move names around to get the right mix of people at each table. Small Post-it® notes also work wonderfully for this. We were each in charge of placing our own friends and relatives. Wedding planning books suggest seating immediate families nearest the bride and groom and lively people who love to dance near the band and DJ, and everything else will fall into place. Wrong!

Setting up a viable seating plan is like trying to piece together a jigsaw puzzle. Savvy guests understand that the farther away they are from the head table, the less status they have in the eyes of the bride or groom and their families. For this reason, some couples avoid having a head table. Loud music can be offensive to some and enjoyable to others. It's hard to sort out who's not speaking to whom, or to find appropriate people who can tolerate sitting with a cranky aunt or a groping uncle. And won't it cause tension to place divorcing couples at a table with happy ones? Or newly remarried or engaged couples at tables with their ex-husbands or old boyfriends?

We argued over where to put my ex-husband and his wife. You guessed it. They ended up at the next table (but only because he was escorting an aunt who had been like a grandmother to my children). Sometimes we have to swallow hard lumps, but they do go down if we drink enough wine.

If yours will be a stand-up cocktail party, you are still not home free. You'll need to consider reserved seating for elderly guests, who will want to park at a table for the duration of the event. Choose spots near a doorway that will allow them to make their way easily to the restrooms.

The bride and groom have the final say on who sits where. You may have input if you've put money where your mouth is.

Out-of-town arrivals

The hubbub begins the day before the wedding. You may or may not be involved with relatives and good friends who have traveled from afar to share your daughter's or son's special day. Depending on the situation, such guests may expect you to pick them up at the airport or shuttle them around to their hotel and events. If you have thought this through on your time schedule, you've arranged to have someone else tend to these needs. Unburden your immediate family as much as possible from the responsibility of tending to guests. Suggest those guests with families rent a car. Are they looking for a meal? You may need to cook dinner, provide it via take-out, or suggest a restaurant. My brother arranged for a hospitality room to be set up at the hotel where everyone was staying. It offered beverages, cold cuts, and salads.

Just stress or The End?

It's common for the bride or groom to get cold feet at the final hour. For many of us mothers, it's hard to remember what it was like to begin a new life; the sheer terror of possible failure and taking on the responsibility for someone else. If your child comes to you teary-eyed and hesitant, try to determine if the upset is caused by a legitimate issue about the marriage, or if it is just the jitters. Hug him or her and squeeze out the real concerns.

If it turns out to be your worst nightmare—there is a problem with the relationship and it should be ended—*lie*. Tell your son or daughter that you don't care about canceling the wedding, as long as he or she is positive that it is the right move. Breaking off a wedding is less painful and expensive than filing for a divorce later on. If there is time, delay calling around with the news until the situation has settled a bit. The two lovers may return hand in hand announcing they changed their minds. It happens more often than not.

The rehearsal

The prenuptial rehearsal signals the start of the wedding rollout. While this is a serious prelude to the wedding, it's okay to have a little fun to lighten the mood. Nerves are on edge. It's time to relax and enjoy the upcoming wedding rituals as they unfold.

Any wedding requiring a significant amount of work requires a rehearsal. The purpose of a rehearsal is to be sure everyone who will take part in the ceremony understands what is going to take place, and what his or her role will be. With a little luck, the practice may prevent embarrassing gaffs in front of the throng of guests. The process is a pretend ceremony, and the orchestrator is the pastor, reverend, rabbi, or justice of the peace who will officiate at the real ceremony. The rehearsal often takes place the evening before the wedding, because at that time all attendants and people who will participate should be available.

This is a grand time for introductions and for finalizing the line-up for the procession. The singer, organist or instrumentalists, and any folks doing readings or participating in the ceremony in any way should be present. If you will have small children as ring bearers or flower girls, ask their parents to attend. The little ones may feel shy at first, but a few practice walks down the aisle should make them comfortable.

To simulate the ceremony, use staging props. An old-fashioned tradition is for the bride to carry a faux bouquet made up of bows from the bridal shower, punched into a paper plate. We brought along a Burger King crown for the groom to wear. Have a pillow for the ring bearer, and give the flower girl pretend flowers. If you will provide a unity candle, bring it to the facility at this time, so it will be in place for the following day. The florist will take care of flower arrangements, so don't worry about this now.

You've coaxed your son into staying at the house after the rehearsal dinner. He's had his own place for quite a while, and he doesn't live home anymore. You change the sheets in his childhood room and pick some white flowers for the dresser and pretend he's yours for one last time. Your son. You feel as if you're losing him, yet sanity tells you that isn't true. His wife, your new "daughter," will be a wonderful and loving addition to your family.

So what's your problem? Are you jealous? No of course not. Maybe you are just worried that this wedding week will be the last time you get to spend time alone with your son. Daughters, you can sneak away with on the guise of shopping and doing women's stuff; but what excuse do you have to gain time alone with your son? You're not a golfer, nor a bowler. And you hate sports. So maybe you are losing him, just a little. Your baby boy.

Dear Joy,

I thought I'd already handled the hard part, but I forgot about my emotions. Am I losing a child?

CHAPTER 14

The Big Day

WHEN YOU AWAKEN THE MORNING of the wedding, you'll feel a strange calmness. It also might be that you have a slight hangover from the festivities of the previous evening. Once we've passed the rehearsal dinner stage, we can finally relax and reap the rewards of our efforts. If you have an evening wedding, as we did, the whole day stretches languidly before you. If the wedding is this morning, you'd better get up and get everyone moving!

The mother in you will, I'm sure, make certain that all the little chickens fluttering around your home during the day are eating properly. The excitement will be wherever the bride and groom are. If your son or daughter is getting ready somewhere else, grab your family and go there or you will miss out on the best part of the day. Don't be pests, though. Do what you can to help ease the confusion and stress levels of everyone involved. Send one of the men out for bagels or donuts or go yourself. Serve juice and coffee, but go easy on the caffeine if the stress level is high.

We lit lavender candles, guaranteed by aroma therapists to reduce stress. If you do this, assign someone to blow them out before you leave. I mended a broken bridesmaid strap, hooked clasps on necklaces, and told all the girls they looked beautiful. Before my son's wedding, my husband helped the groomsmen tie their bow ties, and I checked their tuxes for cat hairs before they left for the ceremony. Offer nothing but compliments on this wonderful day and there will be no room for much else but smiles.

It's common for those who have not been "living" the wedding for many months to feel nervous. My husband broke into a cold sweat and some of the bridesmaids felt nauseous. With my son, I hadn't been directly involved, so the jitters hit us all at the same time. We laughed, went to the bar, and served ourselves shots of tequila. Immediate calm. A single tot of liquor won't make you drunk when you are this revved up, believe me.

As everyone is getting ready, get out your camera and snap photos. I have a cute shot of my two daughters wearing "Jolene®" mustaches, and great candid shots of my son and his groomsmen, just back from the golf course. Many men relieve tension through sports. You'll enjoy these photos in the years to come.

It's easy to get sappy about losing your child to marriage, but don't pass it on. The last thing your child needs from you today is a guilt trip. Transfer your emotions onto paper and then tuck them away; you'll be able to unburden yourself without involving others who might become upset. (Now you know what makes us writers tick!) You *are* allowed to become emotional when you give your daughter the hand-tatted handkerchief you've been saving for this day, made by your grandmother, or when you present your son with your grandfather's pocket watch.

> *The old lore—something old, something new, something borrowed something blue—holds today. Something old represents eternal friendship; something new, health, happiness, and success; something borrowed brings good luck only if it's returned; and blue signifies fidelity. If you can get your daughter to truck around on the wedding day with a silver sixpence in her shoe, she might enjoy financial security.*[28]

The bridal bouquets and her parents' corsages and boutonnières will be delivered to wherever the bride and her maids are getting ready. The photographer will show up within an hour or so of the wedding to take formal at-home shots. The rest of the corsages and boutonnières are normally delivered to the ceremony site for the groom, best man, ushers, and honored guests.

Where's Dad? As we rushed about the house getting everyone ready for my first daughter's wedding, I noticed my husband, handsomely attired in his tux, sitting on the cat's favorite chair writing furiously. We were hosting this wedding and he was inspired to write a welcome speech for our guests. The speech was so wonderful that it brought many of us to tears, but it took me at least five minutes to brush all the cat hairs off his backside.

Your husband, now in his take-charge mode, will ensure that everything moves along. You'll all need to get to the site by car or by limo—whatever your arrangements. The bride's parents arrive with the wedding party, while the groom's go directly to the ceremony—often in the company of the groom and ushers. The groom and his ushers will need to arrive at the ceremony site at least thirty minutes beforehand, as they are the welcoming committee. They also will need time to don their boutonnières and prepare to hand out corsages to participants and honored guests and programs to all attendees.

The weather is always a worry. No bride wants it to rain on her wedding day. But if we all waited for a sunny day to be married, some of us would be spinsters now. No one can control the weather and bad weather is no omen. It may rain; it may snow; or it may be sweltering hot outdoors. No matter. The wedding will go on, and so will the marriage. Tell your daughter this when she is looking like a fallen princess because rain is tap dancing on the hood of the limo en route to the ceremony. On Linda's wedding day, the ushers were prepared to escort us into the ceremony with a rooftop's worth of umbrellas. By the time we emerged from the ceremony, the sun peeked through the clouds. A gift, for sure.

> *Why is rain on your wedding day lucky?*
> *It is said that a wet knot is harder to untie.*

As the groom's parents, your arrival at the church won't warrant the same fanfare as the bride's entourage, but you *will* turn heads when you are escorted up the aisle to the front rows. Women will ogle your dress and, if it's tight, the men may eye your wiggle. Walk slowly and pretend you are a queen. Once you're seated, you and your dashing "king" will wait with everyone else for the arrival of the bride and her attendants.

When my son came out to stand and wait for his bride at the head of the church—almost within arm's reach of us, I wanted to grab him, hug him, and keep him with me always. But when I saw the glow of happiness in his eyes as his bride appeared in white loveliness to meet him at the altar, I was mentally able to release him to her. I had to. It's a paradox, isn't it? Wanting to hang on by the last thread and knowing you can't. There is so much focus on the bride that it's easy to skim over the emotions surrounding the marriage of a son. We are less prepared to deal with them as, unlike a bride's mother, we haven't been as actively involved in the wedding.

Mother of the Groom

The range of emotions floating through your head is enough to make you bawl your eyes out. You feel the euphoria of the moment and the guilt of the selfish mother in your breast. So you smile and cry at the same time. And manage to look utterly ridiculous. It's bad enough that tears that are dripping in black streaks down your cheeks, but that runny nose is embarrassing. You quietly retrieve a tissue from your dress purse, then give your nose a good honk, while holding your arms close to your sides and keeping your head erect so those behind you will think it's the bride's mother breaking the solemnity of the ceremony. Where is that organ music when you need it?

As the mother of the bride, I had already exhausted the bulk of my emotions by the time I reached the ceremony. If the truth be told, I did go through two packets of tissues, but that's to be expected. By the way, that waterproof eye makeup doesn't hold up past the first sniffle.

Weddings are emotion-packed events that catch us when we are least expecting it. We well up with tears when the bridal party situates on the altar, and are sobbing noisily while the bride and groom speak their vows. It's love, pure and simple, our love for them and for all humanity. I realize, now, that we are weeping for the pure joy of it all. Not only for the couple being married, but for ourselves, for our blessings, for our families, and our good fortune to be here in this one place surrounded by those we love in this single moment in time. There I go again. I can't even write about this without tears filling my eyes.

Suggested contents of a mother's purse:

- Two packets of tissues
- Breath mints to hand out
- Mini camera or cell phone
- Lipstick
- Comb with pick to fluff helmet hair
- Replacement mascara, eyeliner, and eye shadow

- Pressed powder compact with mirror
- A twenty-dollar bill, in case you get stranded somewhere

The events of the wedding will unfold from here. Let them. All the spokes of the wheel are in place and it will move as it should if everyone is doing his or her job. If a problem arises, maybe others can handle it for you. All that matters now is that your child has taken a vow of allegiance you hope will last forever; that they will be happy and content with their lives; and that you will continue to be part of it.

Congrats!

Throwing stuff at the bride and groom as they exit the ceremony has long been a worldwide tradition. There was an old Celtic custom of breaking shortbread over the heads of the bride and groom as they departed the church. Unmarried folks would then scramble to pick up the crumbs from the ground to ensure they too would be successful in finding a life partner. Rice means good luck and hopes for a full pantry. (The rumor that rice swells up bird's stomachs and kills them is hogwash.) Grains or nuts represent life-giving seeds. Some European countries throw eggs[29]. We used to throw confetti, but have switched to rice, bird seed, or rose petals. If you must offer guests a throwable, opt for something biodegradable or edible that won't injure the bride and groom or stain their clothing. Keep in mind, anything you choose will surely leave a mess.

It's common to want to congratulate the bride and groom right after the wedding. Some couples will stop at each pew on their way up the aisle to greet guests, while other will dash by to form a receiving line outside the ceremony. The receiving line may be simple with only the bride and groom, but more often the entire wedding party and the parents of the bride and groom line up to greet and hug everyone. Parents of the bride and groom should stick around after the ceremony for formal wedding party photos.

Having a receiving line immediately following the ceremony, rather than holding off until the reception, is more timely and efficient. Everyone needs to pass through to exit. I always am disappointed when a couple heads right to their limo and puts off greeting guests until the reception, either by formal receiving line or by making the rounds once the party is underway.

Enjoy the celebration

Your next stop is the reception. If the ceremony is at the same spot as the reception, you're already there! We had a two-hour gap between the ceremony and the reception, which couldn't be helped. We needlessly worried about how the guests might fill the time in between. Many went home or to their hotels to rest or to change into fancier attire. We found our relatives from out of town parked at the reception hall's bar and joined them for a visit while the wedding party posed for photos outdoors.

If you are taking a limo to the reception, note that it will now be more crowded, as you have added all the ushers and of course the groom. This is where having a party bus pays off, as there will be plenty of room for everyone. Pack a cooler with champagne and disposable flutes to sip on for the ride to the reception.

From now on, the day will fly. You will be caught up in a round of greeting and visiting with family and friends and will hardly remember eating anything, much less where you left your last drink. This is why it is important to have pictures and, better, a video of the wedding. You will be able to relive the day whenever you wish from the comfort of your favorite chair at home.

Once the wedding party makes its grand entrance and is introduced—this tradition is not always followed in modern day weddings—the dancing begins. First, the bride and groom. They are followed by the rest of the entourage and then joined by wedding guests. Your daughter or son will have picked out meaningful songs for special dances with you or your husband, tearjerkers like "Daddy's Little Girl." These touching moments make this day worth every penny spent.

The cake is a decorative and tasty feature of every wedding. My daughter refused to cut the cake to the traditional song, which if you listen hard is the music to "Three Blind Mice." I say she's lucky that she isn't having the whole thing thrown at her, as they did in Roman times to ensure fertility. Later, kissing over a tall tower of cakes became a game of fortune. If the bride and groom managed the deed without knocking over the cake, they would have a life of good luck. This eventually evolved into cutting the cake to signify sharing their life. Every guest must eat a crumb to ensure good luck, though.[30] So forget your diet and chow down.

The ritual of the groom removing the garter has such sexist overtones that it can be a turnoff for today's bride. The custom originated when a frustrated bride, rather than have drunkards pull it off her, removed her garter and flung it to them. From what I understand, while the modern bride may wear a garter (it's usually got the "something blue" on it), she tosses a fake one.

Bouquet-tossing stemmed from garter-tossing, and we've pretty much held to that. If the bride wants to keep her bouquet, she tosses a bogus one. It is said that whoever catches it will be married next, but does that hold true for fake bouquets? I have been happily married for too many years to count, but I can remember the humiliation of being urged up with all the single women to catch the dang thing. Maybe this is another tradition that should be tossed.

Money and gifts

We never talked about the mother of the bride's tote. This is the large purse you tuck under the table and guard with your life meant to hold envelopes handed to the bride and groom throughout the day. Many of these envelopes will contain cash or checks. While you are up and about, ask Grandma—or someone trustworthy who is not very mobile—to hold on to the goods for you. One never likes to consider theft at such an event, but better to guard against it rather than to encourage a problem. Slotted boxes and all sorts of gismos can be set on a table to hold such envelopes. The box can be picked up and carried away.

Traditionally, a table is set aside for wedding gifts brought to the wedding. These need to leave with you, as well as any bouquets, photographs, or special items you brought to embellish the reception. The clean up after the reception can be exhausting if you haven't assigned such tasks in your schedule. The ushers and bridesmaids will help you load cars, if asked. We had the caterer present us with "doggie" tins of unused dinners. Take these if you feel you can use them. We stayed at a hotel, so had no means of keeping the food fresh. The cake top is also sent home with the bride to eat on the couple's first anniversary. If you aren't watchful, it might live in your freezer indefinitely.

The getaway

Formerly, the bride and groom would sneak away after cutting the cake, but these days most aren't as anxious to consummate the wedding night as they are to stay and enjoy the party. The decorative getaway still exists, though. It's common to see a bride and groom driving away in a car streaming crepe paper ribbons and marked "Just Married" with a soap bar. This, too, has its roots in a custom that involved throwing shoes at the couple's car. If they hit them it meant good luck.[31] Ultimately, people settled for tying shoes to a car's bumper, and you may see that today.

Okay, I know the day is over and what the couple do next is not our concern, but there is one particular custom I read of that's a hoot. We need a little lightening up after a long day, don't we? Have you ever heard of the salmon leap? In order for the groom to join his new wife in bed, he crouches on the floor and then springs onto the bed in a single leap, imitating a salmon swimming upstream to spawn.[32] (I apologize if I've insulted anyone's cultural traditions.)

Sleep well, Mom.

EPILOGUE

*Y*OU BREATHE A SIGH OF *relief that it's over. Yet it's not over. The memories of this day will live on—in pictures, in videos, and in your diminished bank account. Your closet becomes a hanging memorial to your daughter's wedding. A glitzy, purple, mother-of-the-bride or groom dress you'll most likely never wear again drips limply from its hook. The tux and accessories your husband bought when he got sick of renting them, are soldiers waiting for marching orders. But the fluffy couturier wedding gown with the red wine stain down its skirt brings back the wedding day each time you pull back the closet door. You see your daughter dancing happy circles amidst all your favorite people. A vision. It was worth it. Each time you shut that closet door, you do so with a pang of guilt. Someday, you really must get that gown cleaned.*

INDEX

XYZ

ENDNOTES

1   (http://www.weddingdetails.com/lore/native.cfm#hopi), which appears as Wedding Details website; <u>Native American Traditions</u>, Hopi Traditions.

2   (http://www.hudsonvalleyweddings.com/guide/customs.htm), which appears as Beekman Arms. Delmater Inn website, <u>Enduring Wedding Traditions... Customs and Their Origins.</u>

3   (http://en.wikipedia.org/wiki/Bride_kidnapping), which appears as Wikepedia website, <u>Bride Kidnapping</u>, p.1.

4   Gilbran, Kahlil; <u>The Prophet</u>, 37th printing; Alfred A. Knopf, Inc. 2001 (now avail on Kindle).

5   Post, Peggy; *Emily Post's* <u>Wedding Etiquette,</u> 5th Edition, Collins (an imprint of Harper Collins Publishing) 2006.

6   (http://www.weddingdetails.com/lore/african.cfm), which appears as Wedding Details website, <u>African Wedding Traditions</u>, p.3.

7   (http://wedding.theknot.com/wedding-planning/wedding-reception-planning/articles/home-wedding-reception-secrets.aspx?MsdVisit=), which appears as The Knot website, <u>Wedding Receptions: At Home Wedding Secrets.</u>

8   See The Knot, #7.

9   See About, #10.

10 (http://weddings.about.com/od/gettingstarted/a/weddingplanners.htm), which appears as About website, Weddings, <u>What do Wedding Planners Do?</u> (http://weddings.about.com/od/weddingplanners/a/weddingplannerscost.htm), About, <u>How Much Do Wedding Planners Cost?</u>

11 (http://www.weddingbusinesstoday.com/news/wedding-industry-statistics/), which appears as Wedding Business Today website, <u>Wedding Industry Statistics</u>, Chris Jaeger, 2010.

12   (http://www.theweddingreport.com/bz/index.php/who-pays-for-the-wedding-2010/), which appears as The Wedding Report website, <u>Who Pays for the Wedding—2010</u>.

13   (http://www.sane-wedding-planning.com/wedding-costs-breakdown.html), which appears as Sane Wedding Planning website, <u>Wedding Costs Breakdown for the Average Wedding Budget.</u>

14   (http://www.realsimple.com/holidays-entertaining/weddings/budget/wedding-cost-calculator-00000000008302/index.html), which appears as Real Simple website, <u>Wedding Cost Calculator.</u>

15   (http://www.celebrateintimateweddings.com/ceremonybroom.html), which appears as Celebrate Intimate Weddings website, <u>Jumping the Broom</u>, Larry James.

16   (http://www.aboutweddings.com/editorials/re;ated-ed.php?article id=46), About, Weddings, <u>Reception: Space Requirements/the Comfort of Your Guests.</u> (http://dcwed.com/html/article_7.html), which appears as The Washington D.C Wedding Guide website, <u>Setup Ideas and Options for your Wedding Reception</u>, Frank Whyte.

17   Fields, Allan & Denise; <u>Bridal Bargains: Secrets to Throwing a Fantastic Wedding on a Realistic Budget</u>, Windsor Press, 2010.

18   Fields, #17.

19   (http://www.hudsonvalleyweddings.com/guide/customs.htm), which appears as Hudson Valley Weddings website, <u>The Wedding Cake…History, Customs and Traditions</u>, p.2.

20   (http://wedding.theknot.com/wedding-planning/wedding-favors/articles/all-about-jordan-almonds.aspx?MsdVisit=1), The Knot, <u>Wedding Favors: All About Jordon Almonds.</u>

21   (http://www.weddings.co.uk/info/tradsup.htm), which appears as Weddings (uk) website, <u>Wedding Superstitions and Traditions</u>, p.2.

22   Post, #5.

23   Paperlesspost.com; cocodot.com; which appear as Paperless Post and Cocodot websites.

24   (http://ezinearticles.com/?Wedding-Customs-Throughout-History-From-Bridal-Party-To-The-Origin-Of-Engagement-And-Wedding-Rings&id=782331), which appears as Ezine Articles website, Wedding Customs <u>Throughout History from Bridal Party to the Origin of Engagement and Wedding Rings</u>, The Origin of the Wedding Party.

25   (http://itthing.com/wedding-superstitions), which appears as It Thing website, <u>Wedding Superstitions You May Not Know About</u>, The Wedding Dress.

26 Beekman Arms. Delmater Inn, #2.

27   Beekman Arms. Delmater Inn, #2.

28 Beekman Arms. Delmater Inn, #2.

29 Beekman Arms. Delmater Inn, #2.

30 Beekman Arms. Delmater Inn, #2.

31 Beekman Arms. Delmater Inn, #2.

32 Ezine Articles, Celtic Wedding Rites… "Tying the Knot." http://ezinearticles.
com/?Celtic-Wedding-Rituals—Tying-the-knot&id=24737.

REFERENCES

Alan & Denise Fields, *Bridal Bargains: Secrets to Throwing a Fantastic Wedding on a Realistic Budget*, Windsor Peak Press, 2010.

Gilbran, Kahlil; *The Prophet*, 37th printing; Alfred A. Knopf, Inc. 2001 (now avail on Kindle).

Post, Peggy; *Emily Post's Wedding Etiquette*, 5th Edition, Collins (an imprint of Harper Collins Publishing) 2006.

Chabad.org, Jewish Marriage, Secrets of a Successful Second Marriage, Rueven P. Bulka, pgs. 1-5. (http://www.chabad.org/library/article_cdo/aid/336097/jewish/Secrets-to-a-Successful-Second-Marriage.htm).

Divorce.com, Top 10 Reasons Marriages Fail, Pgs. 1-2 (http://www.divorce.com/article/top-10-reasons-marriages-fail).

Marriage-success-secrets.com, Larry Bilotta's Marriage Success Tips, *Top 5 Reasons Why Second Marriages Fail*, pgs.1-3

(http://www.marriage-success-secrets.com/second-marriages.html).

Wedding Industry Statistics 2011, American Wedding Study Brides Magazine (http://weddingindustrystatistics.com/) posted July 5, 2011 by Chris Jaeger.

Wedding Industry Statistics (http://www.weddingbusinesstoday.com/news/wedding-industry-statistics/)

Customs & Traditions:

http://www.weddingdetails.com/lore/native.cfm#hopi)

http://www.debeers.com/bridal/inspiration/the-history-of-engagement-rings/

http://en.wikipedia.org/wiki/Bride_kidnapping

http://www.2.a-weddingday.com/weddings/latinweddings.html

http://www.celebrateintimateweddings.com/ceremonybroom.html

http://www.dobosdelights.com/wedtraditions.htm

http://www.hudsonvalleyweddings.com/guide/customs.htm

http://ezinearticles.com/?Wedding-Myths-and-Superstitions&id=581079

http://itthing.com/wedding-superstitions

http://ezinearticles.com/?Wedding-Customs-Throughout-History-From-Bridal-Party-To-The-Origin-Of-Engagement-And-Wedding-Rings&id=782331

http://ezinearticles.com/?Celtic-Wedding-Rituals----Tying-the-knot&id=24737

www.en.wikipedia.org/wiki/bridal_shower

http://wedding.theknot.com/wedding-planning/wedding-favors/articles/all-about-jordan-almonds.aspx?MsdVisit=1

http://www.weddings.co.uk/info/tradsup.htm

http://wedding.theknot.com/wedding-planning/wedding-favors/articles/all-about-jordan-almonds.aspx?MsdVisit=1

http://www.weddings.co.uk/info/tradsup.htm

On-line Links to Check Out

www.weddingvendors.com

www.theknot.com

http://weddings.about.com

www.en.wikipedia.org/wedding

http://www.pashweddings.com

http://ourmarriage.com/html

http://www.dcwed.com/html/article_7.html (choosing a reception location)

www.projectwedding.com

www.brides.com

www.ourdreamwedding.com

Budgeting:

http://www.sane-wedding-planning.com/wedding-costs-breakdown.html

http://www.betsyraye.com/Costestimatorbreakdown.html

http://www.realsimple.com/holidays-entertaining/weddings/budget/wedding-cost-calculator-00000000008302/index.html (Wedding Cost Calculator by state)

Reception, showers & parties:

http://wedding.theknot.com/wedding-planning/wedding-reception-planning/articles/home-wedding-reception-secrets.aspx?MsdVisit=1

http:///wedding-ideas/wedding-showers-parties/2010/08/Wedding_After_Party_Etiquette_Tips_Advice

http://weddings.about.com/od/showersandparties/a/dayafterbrunch.htm

http://www.projectwedding.com/wedding-ideas/the-post-wedding-brunch-ideas-and-tips

Invitations:

http://www.weddingpaperdivas.com/big-questions-about-wedding-invitations.htm
http://www.projectwedding.com/wedding-ideas/online-wedding-invitations
http://www.greatsavethedatemagnets.com